AA

Pub Walks &
Cycle Rides

The South Downs and the South Coast

Walk routes researched and written by Nick Channer, David Halford, David Hancock, Ann F Stonehouse and Peter Toms.
Cycle routes researched and written by David Foster and Tim Locke
Series managing editor: David Hancock

Produced by AA Publishing
© Automobile Association Developments Limited 2005
First published 2005
Reprinted Mar 2006

Published by AA Publishing (a trading name of Automobile Association Developments Limited, whose registered office is Fanum House, Basing View, Basingstoke, Hampshire RG21 4EA; registered number 1878835).

A02949

Ordnance Survey® This product includes mapping data licensed from Ordnance Survey® with the permission of the Controller of Her Majesty's Stationery Office. © Crown copyright 2006. All rights reserved. Licence number 399221.

ISBN-10: 0-7495-4455-4
ISBN-13: 978-0-7495-4455-3

A CIP catalogue record for this book is available from the British Library.

The contents of this book are believed correct at the time of printing. Nevertheless, the publishers cannot be held responsible for any errors or omissions or for changes in the details given in this book or for the consequences of any reliance on the information it provides. We have tried to ensure accuracy in this book, but things do change and we would be grateful if readers would advise us of any inaccuracies they may encounter. This does not affect your statutory rights.

We have taken all reasonable steps to ensure that these walks and cycle rides are safe and achievable by people with a realistic level of fitness. However, all outdoor activities involve a degree of risk and the publishers accept no responsibility for any injuries caused to readers whilst following these walks and cycle rides. For advice on walking and cycling in safety, see pages 12 to 15.

Visit AA Publishing's website www.theAA.com/bookshop

Page layouts by pentacorbig, High Wycombe
Colour reproduction by Keene Group, Andover
Printed in Spain by Graficas Estella

AA

Pub Walks &
Cycle Rides

The South
Downs
and the
South Coast

Locator map

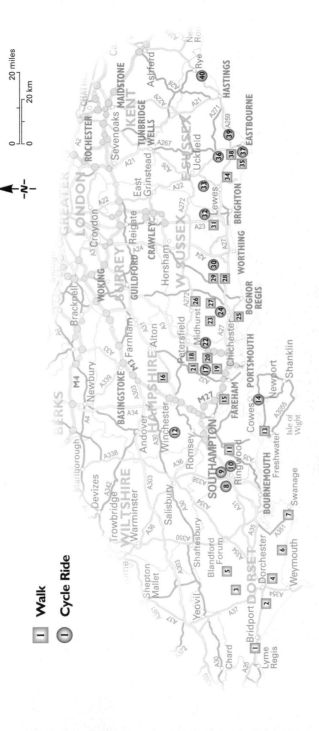

	Walk
	Cycle Ride

Contents

Picture on page 4: Trees near Brockenhurst in the New Forest in Hampshire

Contents

The South Downs and South Coast

This book covers several southern counties, including Dorset, Hampshire, the Isle of Wight and West and East Sussex. Navigating on some walks is made easier by the fact that they follow well-known, waymarked trails such as the South West Coast Path and the South Downs Way. Some cycles routes also follow well-signposted tracks and lanes, such as the Cuckoo Trail which takes you to Michelham Priory and a working watermill, and the Centurion Way. The route, which starts in Chichester, follows the trackbed of a former railway, as does a Hampshire cycle which follows the old Andover to Romsey line.

If it's nature you are after then choose from one of several routes in The New Forest, which offer the chance to see (and hopefully not run into) animals such as the indigenous New Forest ponies (3,500 at the last count), deer and pigs which all roam freely across the forest and the roads. There's plenty of greenery too, as the south of England is home to some of the best unspoiled deciduous forest in western Europe and one of the walks in this book skirts the largest yew forest in Europe. This part of the country is not known for high hills, although some routes involve a leg-stretch to a peak, such as Old Winchester Hill on the South Downs Way near Meonstoke. For fantastic panoramic views, head to the open downland of Devil's Dyke.

As you would expect, there are many coastal walks, including one by the spectacular coastline of Lulworth Cove in Dorset. The geological significance of these cliff exposures, which stretch to east Devon, has led to them being granted World Heritage status. Riverside walks include the pretty Cuckmere River in Sussex.

Many routes have an extra dimension, as they pass places of major historical significance. Southwick village has D-Day connections because Operation Overlord was planned from Southwick House, a house taken over by the Ministry of Defence during the war. Stretching back further in time, you can combine your day out with a visit to Bignor Roman Villa in Sussex or to

the Queen Elizabeth Country Park in Hampshire which has a full-scale recreation of an Iron Age settlement. Two routes take you close to the mysterious chalk outline of the Cerne Abbas Giant near the village of the same name. For castle buffs, choose between Pevensey Castle (which has been in use for more than 1,600 years), the magnificent castle in the attractive Sussex town of Arundel or romantic, ruined Corfe Castle in Dorset.

If you have children in your group, a ride on a steam train on the Watercress Line in Hampshire is guaranteed to please, while a woodland walk in Sussex will take you to the Weald and Downland Open Air Museum. The charming village of Amberley with its thatched and half-timbered houses, has the added attraction of Amberley Working Museum nearby. In good weather you may have to drag yourself away from delightful pubs such as The Castle Inn in West Lulworth (with prize-winning gardens), and The Royal Oak in Cerne Abbas, both in Dorset. Further east, the featured pub in Chalton, The Red Lion, has the distinction of being the oldest pub in Hampshire.

Below: Cliffs at Mupe Bay in Dorset

Using this book

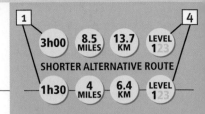

MAP: OS Explorer OL24 White Peak
START/FINISH: Rudyard Old Station, grid ref SJ 955579
TRAILS/TRACKS: old railway trackbed
LANDSCAPE: wooded lake shore, peaceful pastures and meadows
PUBLIC TOILETS: Rudyard village
TOURIST INFORMATION: Leek, tel 01538 483741
CYCLE HIRE: none near by
THE PUB: The Abbey Inn, Leek, see Directions to the pub, page 27
❶ Take care along the banks of the lake – keep well away from the shore line

Each walk and cycle ride has a coloured panel giving essential information for the walker and cyclist, including the distance, terrain, nature of the paths, and where to park your car.

1 **MINIMUM TIME:** The time stated for completing each route is the estimated minimum time that a reasonably fit family group of walkers or cyclists would take to complete the circuit. This does not allow for rest or refreshment stops.

2 **MAPS:** Each route is shown on a detailed map. However, some detail is lost because of the restrictions imposed by scale, so for this reason, we recommend that you use the maps in conjunction with a more detailed Ordnance Survey map. The relevant Ordnance Survey Explorer map appropriate for each walk or cycle is listed.

3 **START/FINISH:** Here we indicate the start location and parking area. There is a six-figure grid reference prefixed by two letters showing which 100km square of the National Grid it refers to. You'll find more information on grid references on most Ordnance Survey maps.

4 **LEVEL OF DIFFICULTY:** The walks and cycle rides have been graded simply (1 to 3) to give an indication of their relative difficulty. Easier routes, such as those with little total ascent, on easy footpaths or level trails, or those covering shorter distances are graded 1. The hardest routes, either because they include a lot of ascent, greater distances, or are in hilly, more demanding terrains, are graded 3.

5 **TOURIST INFORMATION:** The nearest tourist information office and contact number is given for further local information, in particular opening details for the attractions listed in the 'Where to go from here' section.

6 **CYCLE HIRE:** We list, within reason, the nearest cycle hire shop/centre.

7 ❶ Here we highlight any potential difficulties or dangers along the route. At a glance you will know if the walk is steep or crosses difficult terrain, or if a cycle route is hilly, encounters a main road, or whether a mountain bike is essential for the off-road trails. If a particular route is suitable for older, fitter children we say so here.

About the pub

Generally, all the pubs featured are on the walk or cycle route. Some are close to the start/finish point, others are at the midway point, and occasionally, the recommended pub is a short drive from the start/finish point. We have included a cross-section of pubs, from homely village locals and isolated rural gems to traditional inns and upmarket country pubs which specialise in food. What they all have in common is that they serve food and welcome children.

The description of the pub is intended to convey its history and character and in the 'food' section we list a selection of dishes, which indicate the style of food available. Under 'family facilities', we say if the pub offers a children's menu or smaller portions of adult dishes, and whether the pub has a family room, highchairs, baby-changing facilities, or toys. There is detail on the garden, terrace, and any play area.

DIRECTIONS: If the pub is very close to the start point we state see Getting to the Start. If the pub is on the route the relevant direction/map location number is given, in addition to general directions. In some cases the pub is a short drive away from the finish point, so we give detailed directions to the pub from the end of the route.

PARKING: The number of parking spaces is given. All but a few of the walks and rides start away from the pub. If the pub car park is the parking/start point, then we have been given permission by the landlord to print the fact. You should always let the landlord or a member of staff know that you are using the car park before setting off.

OPEN: If the pub is open all week we state 'daily' and if it's open throughout the day we say 'all day', otherwise we just give the days/sessions the pub is closed.

FOOD: If the pub serves food all week we state 'daily' and if food is served throughout the day we say 'all day', otherwise we just give the days/sessions when food is not served.

BREWERY/COMPANY: This is the name of the brewery to which the pub is tied or the pub company that owns it. 'Free house' means that the pub is independently owned and run.

REAL ALE: We list the regular real ales available on handpump. 'Guest beers' indicates that the pub rotates beers from a number of microbreweries.

DOGS: We say if dogs are allowed in pubs on walk routes and detail any restrictions.

ROOMS: We list the number of bedrooms and how many are en suite. For prices please call the pub.

Please note that pubs change hands frequently and new chefs are employed, so menu details and facilities may change at short notice. Not all the pubs featured in this guide are listed in the *AA Pub Guide*. For information on those that are, including AA-rated accommodation, and for a comprehensive selection of pubs across Britain, please refer to the *AA Pub Guide* or see the AA's website www.theAA.com

Alternative refreshment stops

At a glance you will see if there are other pubs or cafés along the route. If there are no other places on the route, we list the nearest village or town where you can find somewhere else to eat and drink.

☛ Where to go from here

Many of the routes are short and may only take a few hours. You may wish to explore the surrounding area after lunch or before tackling the route, so we have selected a few attractions with children in mind.

Walking and cycling in safety

WALKING

All the walks are suitable for families, but less experienced family groups, especially those with younger children, should try the shorter or easier walks first. Route finding is usually straightforward, but the maps are for guidance only and we recommend that you always take the suggested Ordnance Survey map with you.

Risks

Although each walk has been researched with a view to minimising any risks, no walk in the countryside can be considered to be completely free from risk. Walking in the outdoors will always require a degree of common sense and judgement to ensure that it is as safe as possible, especially for young children.

- Be particularly careful on cliff paths and in upland terrain, where the consequences of a slip can be serious.

- Remember to check tidal conditions before walking on the seashore.
- Some sections of route are by, or cross, busy roads. Remember traffic is a danger even on minor country lanes.
- Be careful around farmyard machinery and livestock.
- Be aware of the consequences of changes in the weather and check the forecast before you set out. Ensure the whole family is properly equipped, wearing warm clothing and a good pair of boots or sturdy walking shoes. Take waterproof clothing with you and carry spare clothing and a torch if you are walking in the winter months. Remember the weather can change quickly at any time of the year, and in moorland and heathland areas, mist and fog can make route finding much harder. In summer, take account of the heat and sun by wearing a hat and carrying enough water.

- On walks away from centres of population you should carry a whistle and survival bag. If you do have an accident requiring emergency services, make a note of your position as accurately as possible and dial 999.

CYCLING

Cycling is a fun activity which children love, and teaching your child to ride a bike, and going on family cycling trips, are rewarding experiences. Not only is cycling a great way to travel, but as a regular form of exercise it can make an invaluable contribution to a child's health and fitness, and increase their confidence and sense of independence.

The growth of motor traffic has made Britain's roads increasingly dangerous and unattractive to cyclists. Cycling with children is an added responsibility and, as with everything, there is a risk when taking them out for a day's cycling. However, in recent years many measures have been taken to address this, including the on-going development of the National Cycle Network (8,000 miles utilising quiet lanes and traffic-free paths) and local designated off-road routes for families, such as converted railway lines, canal towpaths and forest tracks.

In devising the cycle rides in this guide, every effort has been made to use these designated cycle paths, or to link them with quiet country lanes and waymarked byways and bridleways. Unavoidably, in a few cases, some relatively busy B-roads have been used to link the quieter, more attractive routes.

Rules of the road
- Ride in single file on narrow and busy roads.
- Be alert, look and listen for traffic, especially on narrow lanes and blind bends and be extra careful when descending steep hills, as loose gravel can lead to an accident.
- In wet weather make sure you keep a good distance between you and other riders.
- Make sure you indicate your intentions clearly.
- Brush up on *The Highway Code* before venturing out on to the road.

Off-road safety code of conduct
- Only ride where you know it is legal to do so. It is forbidden to cycle on public footpaths, marked in yellow. The only 'rights of way' open to cyclists are bridleways (blue markers) and unsurfaced tracks, known as byways, which are open to all traffic and waymarked in red.
  - Canal towpaths: you need a permit to cycle on some stretches of towpath (www.waterscape.com). Remember that access paths can be steep and slippery and always get off and push your bike under low bridges and by locks.

- Always yield to walkers and horses, giving adequate warning of your approach.
- Don't expect to cycle at high speeds.
- Keep to the main trail to avoid any unnecessary erosion to the area beside the trail and to prevent skidding, especially if it is wet.
- Remember the Country Code.

Cycling with children
Children can use a child seat from the age of eight months, or from the time they can hold themselves upright. There are a number of child seats available which fit on the front or rear of a bike and towable two-seat trailers are worth investigating. 'Trailer bicycles', suitable for five- to ten-year-olds, can be attached to the rear of an adult's bike, so that the adult has control, allowing the child to pedal if he/she wishes. Family cycling can be made easier by using a tandem, as it can carry a child seat and tow trailers. 'Kiddy-cranks' for shorter legs can be fitted to the rear seat tube, enabling either parent to take their child out cycling. With older children it is better to purchase the right size bike rather than one that is too big, as an oversized bike will be difficult to control, and potentially dangerous.

Preparing your bicycle
A basic routine includes checking the wheels for broken spokes or excess play in the bearings, and checking the tyres for punctures, undue wear and the correct tyre pressures. Ensure that the brake blocks are firmly in place and not worn, and that cables are not frayed or too slack. Lubricate hubs, pedals, gear mechanisms and cables. Make sure you have a pump, a bell, a rear rack to carry panniers and, if cycling at night, a set of working lights.

Preparing yourself
Equipping the family with cycling clothing need not be an expensive exercise. Comfort is the key when considering what to wear. Essential items for well-being on a bike are padded cycling shorts, warm stretch leggings (avoid tight-fitting and seamed trousers like jeans or baggy tracksuit trousers that may become caught in the chain), stiff-soled training shoes, and a wind and waterproof jacket. Fingerless gloves will add to your comfort.

A cycling helmet provides essential protection if you fall off your bike, so they are particularly recommended for young children learning to cycle.

Wrap your child up with several layers in colder weather. Make sure you and those with you are easily visible by car drivers and other road users, by wearing light-coloured or luminous clothing in daylight and reflective strips or sashes in failing light and when it is dark.

What to take with you

Invest in a pair of medium-sized panniers (rucksacks are unwieldy and can affect balance) to carry the necessary gear for you and your family for the day. Take extra clothes with you, the amount depending on the season, and always pack a light wind/waterproof jacket. Carry a basic tool kit (tyre levers, adjustable spanner, a small screwdriver, puncture repair kit, a set of Allen keys) and practical spares, such as an inner tube, a universal brake/gear cable, and a selection of nuts and bolts. Also, always take a pump and a strong lock.

Cycling, especially in hilly terrain and off-road, saps energy, so take enough food and drink for your outing. Always carry plenty of water, especially in hot and humid weather conditions. Consume high-energy snacks like cereal bars, cake or fruits, eating little and often to combat feeling weak and tired. Remember that children get thirsty (and hungry) much more quickly than adults so always have food and diluted juices available for them.

And finally, the most important advice of all–enjoy yourselves!

USEFUL CYCLING WEBSITES

NATIONAL CYCLE NETWORK
A comprehensive network of safe and attractive cycle routes throughout the UK.
It is co-ordinated by the route construction charity Sustrans with the support of more than 450 local authorities and partners across Britain. For maps, leaflets and more information on the designated off-road cycle trails across the country contact
www.sustrans.org.uk
www.nationalcyclenetwork.org.uk

LONDON CYCLING CAMPAIGN
Pressure group that lobbies MPs, organises campaigns and petitions in order to improve cycling conditions in the capital. It provides maps, leaflets and information on cycle routes across London.
www.lcc.org.uk

BRITISH WATERWAYS
For information on towpath cycling, visit
www.waterscape.com

FORESTRY COMMISSION
For information on cycling in Forestry Commission woodland see
www.forestry.gov.uk/recreation

CYCLISTS TOURING CLUB
The largest cycling club in Britain, provides information on cycle touring, and legal and technical matters
www.ctc.org.uk

From Seatown to Golden Cap

WALK

Seatown

DORSET

Climb a fine top, owned by one of the country's most popular charities.

Golden Cap

Golden Cap is the rather obvious name for a high, flat-topped hill of deep orange sandstone on the cliffs between Charmouth and Bridport. It represents the tail end of a vein of the warm-coloured sandstone that stretches down from the Cotswolds. The Cap is the highest point on the south coast, at 627ft (191m), with views along the shore to the tip of Portland Bill in one direction and to Start Point in the other. Inland, you can see Pilsdon Pen and as far as the heights of Dartmoor.

Climbing towards the top, you pass from neat fields, through a line of wind-scoured oak trees, into an area of high heathland, walking up through bracken, heather, bilberry and blackberry, alive with songbirds. The loose undercliff on the seaward side creates a different habitat. In botanical and wildlife terms, Golden Cap is one of the richest properties in the National Trust's portfolio. Today we tend to associate the National Trust with the upkeep of grand houses but, in fact, its first acquisition, way back in 1896, was a stretch of coast in Wales. Today the charity is one of Britain's biggest private landowners.

On the very top of Golden Cap itself is a simple memorial to the Earl of Antrim, chairman of the Trust in the 1960s and 1970s. It was he who spearheaded its 1965 appeal campaign, named 'Enterprise Neptune', to purchase sections of unspoiled coastline before the developers moved in and it was all too late. Golden Cap was part of this and over the years the Trust has continued to buy up pockets of land all around, with the aim of preserving the traditional field pattern that exists in the area between Eype and Lyme Regis.

what to look for

The National Trust owns the ruined church of St Gabriel's (little more than a low shell with a porch to one side) and the neighbouring row of thatched cottages that have been smartly refurbished and are let out as visitor accommodation. They are all that remains of the fishing village of Stanton, sheltering in the valley behind the cliffs, which was largely abandoned after the coast road was rerouted inland in 1824.

the walk

1 Walk back up through Seatown. Cross a stile on the left, on to the footpath, signposted **'Coast Path Diversion'**. Cross a stile at the end, bear left to cross a stile and footbridge into **woodland**. Cross a stile at the other side, go through a gate and bear right up the hill, signposted **'Golden Cap'**.

2 Where the track forks by a **seat** keep left. Go through some trees and over a stile. Bear left, straight across the open hillside, with Golden Cap ahead of you. Pass through a line of trees and walk steeply uphill beside the **fence**. Go up some steps, cross a stile and continue ahead. At the **fingerpost** go left through a gate to follow the path of **shallow steps** up through bracken, heather, bilberry and bramble to the top of Golden Cap.

3 For a short cut, return back down the steps and through the gate. Proceed straight ahead to a stile in the hedge, then follow the field edge to a gate and Point 6. For the longer walk, pass the **trig point** and turn right along the top. Pass the stone

The view of Charmouth and Lyme Regis from Golden Cap

2h30 — **4 MILES** — **6.4 KM** — **LEVEL 123**

WALK

MAP: OS Explorer 116 Lyme Regis & Bridport
START/FINISH: car park (fee) above gravel beach, Seatown – beware, can flood in stormy weather; grid ref: SY 420917
PATHS: field tracks, country lanes, steep zig-zag gravel path, 7 stiles
LANDSCAPE: windswept coastline of lumps and bumps
PUBLIC TOILETS: at end of road, Seatown
TOURIST INFORMATION: Bridport, tel: 01308 424901
THE PUB: The Anchor Inn, Seatown
🅟 Long, steep ascent to the top of Golden Cap; steep descent on longer loop; suitable for fit, older children

Getting to the start

To reach Seatown, take the signed lane opposite the church in Chideock, a small village on the A35 between Bridport and Lyme Regis, 3 miles (4.8km) west of Bridport. Arrive early in summertime to ensure a spave in the car park.

Researched and written by:
David Hancock, Ann F Stonehouse

Seatown DORSET

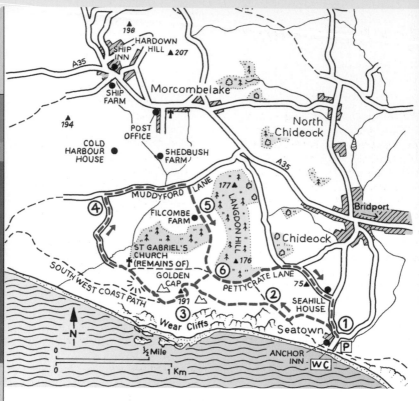

memorial to the Earl of Antrim. At a **marker stone** turn right and follow the zig-zag path steeply downhill, enjoying great views along the bay to Charmouth and Lyme Regis. Go through a gate and bear right over the field towards the ruined **St Gabriel's Church**. In the bottom corner turn down through a gate, passing the ruins on your right, then go through a second gate. Go down the track, passing **cottages** on the left, and bear right towards the access lane.

4 Ignore the Coast Path sign left, and turn right before crossing the stream to follow a waymarked path parallel with the **stream** and beside **St Gabriel's Wood**. The path steepens beyond the wood as you follow the edge of two fields towards farm buildings. Soon cross a stile and turn right along the concrete lane to **Filcombe Farm**.

5 Follow **blue markers** through the farmyard, bearing left through two gates. Walk up the track, go through two more gates and bear left over the top of the green saddle between Langdon Hill and Golden Cap.

6 Go left through a gate in the corner and down a gravel lane (**Pettycrate Lane**) beside the woods, signed 'Seatown'. Ignore a footpath off to the right. At a junction of tracks keep right, downhill, with a delectable green patchwork of fields on the hillside ahead. Pass **Seahill House** on the left and turn right, on to a road. Continue down the road into Seatown to return to your car.

The Anchor Inn

about the pub

The Anchor Inn
Seatown, Chideock
Bridport, Dorset DT6 6JU
Tel: 01297 489215

DIRECTIONS: above the car park at the start of the walk
PARKING: 20
OPEN: daily, all day Easter–September, and Friday, Saturday and Sunday in winter
FOOD: daily, all day Easter–September and winter weekends
BREWERY/COMPANY: Palmers Brewery
REAL ALE: Palmers IPA, 200 and Copper Ale
DOGS: welcome on a lead

The Anchor has a spectacular setting in a little cove surrounded by National Trust land, beneath Golden Cap and with lovely cliff and sea views . It is right on the Dorset coastal path (ideal for walkers), and the inn makes the most of its position with a large sun terrace and cliff-side beer garden overlooking the beach. On winter weekdays it is blissfully quiet, while the summer sees it thronging with holidaymakers. The rusted anchor outside belonged to the Hope, which was wrecked on Chesil Beach during a storm in January 1748, while returning from Curaçao to Amsterdam. Inside are two homely bars with open fires and old photos of the pub and cove, and tip-top real ale from Palmers Brewery in nearby Bridport.

Food

A wide-ranging menu offers something for everyone, from sandwiches (try the excellent crab), burgers and jacket potatoes to prime rump steak. There's plenty of freshly caught seafood, including crab and lobster, and game in season. Typical dishes are monkfish in Thai sauce, game casserole, carbonade of beef, and vegetable and spinach pancakes.

Family facilities

Children are welcome in the family room away from the bar.

☛ Where to go from here

Lyme Regis is a pretty old harbour town, with a landmark breakwater, the Cobb, and crumbling cliffs famous for their fossils – learn more at Dinosaurland fossil museum in the town.

A circuit from Abbotsbury

2

WALK

Abbotsbury DORSET

A walk to a high vantage point above Abbotsbury, where Admiral Nelson's fighting companion is remembered.

Nelson's fighting companion

Admiral Hardy is remembered as the close friend of Admiral Lord Horatio Nelson, who attended the great naval hero in the hour of his death after the Battle of Trafalgar. He was a hero in his own right, his features decorating jugs and tankards of the time. Compared to his literary namesake, you'll

find few memorials to this Hardy in his home county, but there is one monument – and it's a big one. High on Black Down hill, the Hardy Monument looks like a Victorian chimney. You can climb up inside on summer weekends and the views from here over a sea of green fields and down to Portland are superb.

Thomas Masterman Hardy was born in 1769 at Kingston Russell, and from the age of nine was raised in Portesham. Aged 15 he ran away to sea, where he served before the mast and in the galley before enlisting.

In 1796 he was in charge of a captured foreign vessel when he saw two frigates under Nelson's command in danger from a

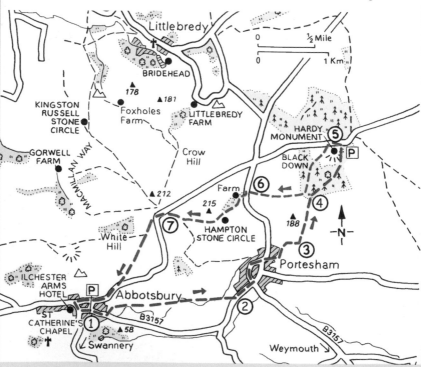

panish squadron. Courageously, Hardy hoisted the British flag, drawing the Spanish fire. He was captured in the ensuing fracas, but was later returned in an exchange of prisoners. Some months later he and Nelson were involved in another near-death adventure, when Nelson stopped the flight of his ship to wait for Hardy, who had gone to the rescue of a drowning seaman. His surprised Spanish pursuers stopped in their tracks.

Hardy became the captain of Nelson's flagships and served with him at his most famous battles. In 1805, as captain of HMS Victory, he was at Nelson's side in that man's greatest hour and when Nelson was mortally wounded. Hardy stayed in the navy for another 30 years. His final service was as Governor of Greenwich Hospital, where he died in 1839.

the walk

1 Return to the car park entrance and turn right. Pass the **Rising Sun** and cross the road to follow the pavement in front of thatched cottages. Just past **Abbotsbury Glebe** take the waymarked old railway path left, signed to Portesham. Keep left beside a house called **Abbots Peace**, pass a stone barn and follow the old track bed for 1.5 miles (2.4km) to the **B3157** on the edge of Portesham.

2 Turn left and join the pavement in a few yards. At the road junction by the **King's Arms** turn left and take care as you walk through the village, passing the stores

The ruins of St Catherine's Chapel on the hill, across the fish pond in Abbotsbury

3h00 — **6.25 MILES** — **10.1 KM** — **LEVEL 1 2 3**

MAP: OS Explorer OL15 Purbeck & South Dorset

START/FINISH: village pay-and-display car park, Abbotsbury; grid ref: SY 578853

PATHS: field tracks, quiet roads, woodland tracks, 6 stiles

LANDSCAPE: rolling hills and escarpments above Abbotsbury

PUBLIC TOILETS: Back Street, Abbotsbury

TOURIST INFORMATION: Bridport, tel: 01398 424901

THE PUB: The Ilchester Arms, Abbotsbury

❗ One steep climb out of Portesham; care to be taken along village road through Portesham; suitable for older family groups.

Getting to the start

Abbotsbury is situated on the B3157 between Weymouth and Bridport, 10 miles (16.1km) north west of Weymouth. The car park is well signposted as you enter the village from Weymouth.

Researched and written by:
David Hancock, Ann F Stonehouse

and post office. Soon take the waymarked bridleway right, signed '**Hardy's Monument**'. Go through a gate and keep left steeply uphill on a track through a line of trees. Follow the wall right and pause at the top of the field for good views across Portesham and out to sea.

3 Turn left into the next field, following the field edge right to a gate. Continue down the field edge (**Hardy's Monument** visible ahead), soon to bear off right to a gate and junction of paths. Turn left and follow the track downhill towards a **ruined stone building** and coniferous woodland. At the first junction by the old building, turn right signposted '**Smitten Corner**'.

4 Begin to climb through the wood, keeping ahead at a crossing of paths. Continue ahead where a track merges from the left, follow the path left then round a right curve. Ignore the grassy track left. At a staggered crossing of paths, take the stony path left. Head uphill through bracken and soon reach **Hardy's Monument** and magnificent all-round views.

5 Turn left down a path by the entrance, signposted '**Inland Route**'. Follow the broad track down through the woods. At the bottom turn right and bear left, before a gate, over a stile. Walk up the edge of two fields. At the corner go over a **stone stile** and immediately cross another. Walk alongside the fence to the hedge and a stile.

6 Turn left on to the road and right towards a **farm** and gate. After passing the farm bear left through a gate and go up a track, then through another gate and bear right. Pass **Hampton Stone Circle** and keep straight on. Cross a stile, walk beside the fence and down some steps, signposted '**West Bexington**'. Follow the path along the hillside and up through a gate to a road.

Signpost on the walk, showing the directions of Abbotsbury and Lime Kiln car park

7 Turn left and soon bear right through a gate on to a bridleway, signed '**West Bexington and Abbotsbury**'. Keep straight ahead along the line of the fence. At the brow of the hill go through a gate and continue ahead and downhill, following a track in the grass. Go through a gate and carry on down. At a crossing of tracks keep straight on, signed 'Abbotsbury'. Go through a gate on to the road and turn right down into the village. At a junction, keep head to the village centre and the **Ilchester Arms**. Turn left, then left at the sharp bend to return to the car park.

what to look for

There is a stone circle on this route, its purpose and origin obscure. It is called the Hampton Stone Circle, where the nine flinty stone lumps (they look like concrete aggregate) are well used by cattle as scratching posts. The stone is a natural phenomenon, with flint gravel cemented by silica, laid down over 40 million years ago.

Take a stroll round Abbotsbury, a lovely village of golden stone, sheltered from the sea by the Fleet and dominated in the landscape by the solitary St Catherine's Chapel, alone on its hill. An abbey was founded here in the time of King Cnut. Dissolution in the 16th century left it a cathedral, one of the biggest tithe barns in England, and a unique swannery.

The Ilchester Arms

The Ilchester Arms comes high on the list of places to visit in this most picturesque of Dorset villages, especially after this walk or a visit to the famous Swannery, the sub-tropical gardens or the ancient St Catherine's Chapel. It's a rambling 16th-century coaching inn that dominates the heart of the village. Inside, a civilised and relaxed atmosphere prevails within several beamed, part-panelled and comfortably furnished rooms, replete with easy chairs in front of the fire and a wealth of interesting artefacts. Beyond the airy conservatory restaurant, peaceful outdoor seating can be found on the sheltered patio and lawn, with lovely views towards the chapel on the hill.

Food

Expect a traditional menu featuring pub favourites and a good range of seafood specials, perhaps local bass, crab and lobster.

Family facilities

Children of all ages are very welcome throughout the inn. There's a children's menu, smaller portions of main menu dishes, and high chairs are available.

about the pub

The Ilchester Arms
Market Street, Abbotsbury
Dorchester, Dorset DT3 4JR
Tel: 01305 871243
www.ilchesterarms.co.uk

DIRECTIONS: on the curve of the main street	
PARKING: 50	
OPEN: daily, all day	
FOOD: daily	
BREWERY/COMPANY: Enterprise Inns	
REAL ALE: Gales HSB, Badger Tanglefoot, Courage Best, Greene King Abbot Ale and Old Speckled Hen	
DOGS: welcome in the bar and garden	

Alternative refreshment stops

Abbotsbury is well supplied with tea rooms and the village's other pub, the Rising Sun is close to the car park. There's also the King's Arms in Portesham and during the summer you will find a refreshment van at Hardy's Monument.

☞ Where to go from here

Abbotsbury Swannery is a unique sanctuary. Mute swans have lived on the Fleet lagoon for 600 years, since they were introduced as a food source for the abbey, and their nest site is now protected. Come in April to see them nesting and from mid-May to see cygnets (www.abbotsbury-tourism.co.uk).

From Minterne Magna to Cerne Abbas

A quiet track leading up Little Minterne Hill

A valley walk between two pretty villages to see a famous chalk hill carving.

The Cerne Abbas Giant

The chalk outline of the Cerne Abbas Giant is so familiar that the reality, seen from the hillside opposite rather than above from the air, is a surprise. His proportions change at this shallower angle, and this of course is how he was designed to be seen – all 180ft (55m) of him. Quite when he was made, and by whom, is part of his mystery.

Was he drawn up there by the Romans, a portrait of the demi-god Hercules? Could he be part of a cunning neolithic plan to frighten away potential enemies from a settlement on the hilltop? On the other hand he might be of Celtic origin, for the giant has been linked to a pan handle discovered 12 miles (19km) away on Hod

Hill. Made of bronze, it depicts a naked man clutching a club in one hand and a limp hare in the other. The man has wings and is surrounded by other symbols which identify him as Nodens, a Celtic god of healing and fertility. His features and the angle of his legs suggest close resemblance to the Giant, and place him in the 1st century AD. Whatever the truth, the Giant has been seen as a symbol of fertility for many centuries. Childless women would spend a night of hope on his crotch. The Giant is now fenced to prevent erosion.

The village of Cerne Abbas is a lovely mix of old houses, some half-timbered, some stone, with flint, thatch and brick in evidence. This was once a major staging post on the coaching routes.

St Augustine visited Cerne and preached to the locals on a spot marked by St Augustine's Well. An abbey was founded here in AD 987. Its most famous inhabitant, Aelfric, produced a number of schoolbooks in Anglo-Saxon. The abbey was dissolved in 1539, along with Dorset's other monastic houses, but an imposing gatehouse with overhanging oriel window and carved lions remains, along with other venerable buildings, including an ancient hospital, set around a flowered courtyard.

2h30 · 5.5 MILES · 8.8 KM · LEVEL 1 2 3

the walk

1 Turn right and walk up the road through the village. Pass the **Minterne Estate** board, go round a sharp left-hand curve and turn right through a gate on to a bridleway. Go straight ahead up the hill. At the top go through a gate and bear left. Follow the **blue marker** diagonally up to the right. Go through a gate, walk on past some trees, then bend right, up round a field towards the tree line.

2 Go through the gap, turn left at the T-junction of paths and follow the main path right down through the woods. At the bottom turn left along the road. After a bend take the footpath right, across the field. After a line of trees veer left, towards a **white gate**. Cross a road, pass to the right of a gate, and continue straight on down the field. Pass another white gate then continue ahead on the road. At the end bear right on to the **A352**.

3 Soon cross to the car park for the best view of the Giant. Take the road down to the village and turn left, signposted **'Pottery'**. Turn right by the stream, signposted 'Village Centre'. Continue over a slab bridge and pass an **old mill**. Bear left, to the high street. Turn left, and left again in front of the Royal Oak, to the **church**. Walk up the Old Pitch Market to the Abbey. Turn right into the **churchyard** and bear left, signposted **'Giant's Hill'**. Go through a gate, and bear half-right across the field.

4 Cross a stile, then turn right up some steps. Now follow the path to the left, round the contour of the hill, below a fence.

MAP: OS Explorer 117 Cerne Abbas & Bere Regis

START/FINISH: car park (free) opposite church, Minterne Magna; grid ref: ST 659043

PATHS: country paths and tracks, minor road, main road, 2 stiles

LANDSCAPE: head of Cerne Valley, scattered with old settlements

PUBLIC TOILETS: Cerne Abbas

TOURIST INFORMATION: Dorchester, tel: 01305 267992

THE PUB: The Royal Oak, Cerne Abbas

🛈 Take care crossing the A352; one long downland climb

Getting to the start

Minterne Magna is a small village on the A352 between Dorchester and Sherborne, 8 miles (12.9km) north of Dorchester and 2 miles (3.2km) north of Cerne Abbas. A parking area is signed in the village opposite the church.

Researched and written by:
David Hancock, Ann F Stonehouse

The turf-cut Cerne Abbas Giant is thought to be a fertility symbol

As the path divides, keep right, up the hill, towards the top. Bear left along the ridge, cross a stile by a **fingerpost** and head diagonally left, towards a **barn**.

what to look for

Hidden from the main road behind high stone walls, Minterne House is a large, yellow Victorian pile, built by the Digby family. It is not open to the public, but its magnificent gardens are. Paths weave through a famous collection of rhododendrons and magnolias.

5 At the barn turn left and go down through a gate. Soon turn right through another gate and follow the **bridleway** along the hillside, with views to Minterne Parva. Keep straight ahead at a junction of tracks, then dip down through a gateway above some woods. Keep straight on to go through a gate near the road. Turn left along the grassy track At a **gateway** turn left on to a gravel lane.

6 Directly above **Minterne House** turn left through a small gate and bear right. Go through a gate and bear half-left, downhill. Continue down through several gates and keep right at the **fingerpost** down a broad track. Cross the stream, then walk up past the church to return to the car park.

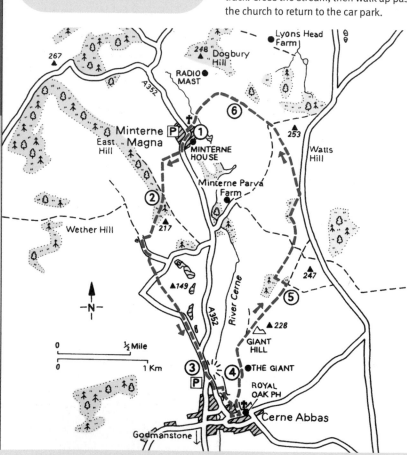

The Royal Oak

Thatched, creeper-clad and situated in a picturesque village below the Dorset Downs, this attractive 16th-century inn was reputedly built out of stone from Cerne's ruined Benedictine Abbey in 1540. Since then it has been a blacksmith's and a coaching inn, and a previous owner of the pub also owned land in America. In 1791 this land was given to the US government, and became the site of Capitol Hill. Hungry walkers, tourists on the Hardy Trail and local diners fill the traditional interior – all flagstones, open log fires, beams and bric-a-brac – in search of excellent real ale and the genuinely home-cooked food that utilises top-notch produce from local suppliers. There's a delightful enclosed courtyard garden with decking and heating for summer eating and drinking.

Food

The imaginative menu takes in classic pub dishes on the 'light bites and walkers' favourites' menu – Blue Vinny ploughman's, open sandwiches, ham, egg and chips – while daily specials may include pan-fried black bream fillets, seafood chowder, venison sausages, whole lemon sole, and local lamb shank with pesto jus.

Family facilities

Children of all ages are welcome inside the pub. Here books and games can be provided, as can smaller portions of the main menu dishes, a menu for younger children, baby-changing facilities and small cutlery. Nothing is too much trouble.

Alternative refreshment stops

In Cerne Abbas you will also find the Red Lion, the New Inn and two tea rooms.

☛ Where to go from here

The nearby village of Godmanstone claims to have the smallest pub in England. The Smith's Arms was a blacksmith's forge, granted a licence on the spot by a thirsty Charles II as he passed through.

about the pub

The Royal Oak
23 Long Street, Cerne Abbas
Dorchester, Dorset DT2 7JG
Tel: 01300 341797

DIRECTIONS: follow signs for the village centre from the A352, the pub is close to the church

PARKING: street parking

OPEN: daily

FOOD: daily

BREWERY/COMPANY: free house

REAL ALE: St Austell Tinners and Tribute, Butcombe, Quay Weymouth Best, Greene King Old Speckled Hen

DOGS: well behaved dogs on leads welcome

The White Horse at Osmington

Osmington

DORSET

Where a sane King George III took a well-earned break.

King George III

Weymouth is a trading port with a patchy history. In the 18th century it was a base for trade with the Americas and the shipping of convicts to Australia. The 1780s saw the emergence of sea bathing (and even seawater drinking) – Weymouth joined in. A royal visit in 1789 rocketed the little town into the top rank of seaside resorts.

Rumours of George III's mental instability threatened to destabilise the country. It was decided that the King should go on a short, highly visible tour to Weymouth, to demonstrate how much better he was. The royal party consisted of the King, the Queen and the three princesses. By the time they reached Weymouth the crowds were ecstatic, with bunting, receptions and gunships firing salutes in the bay. The King

responded to their warmth with a short walk about on his first evening. He declared that he 'never saw a sight so pleasing'.

George III spent ten weeks here on his first visit, enjoying day trips to Lulworth, Milton Abbey and St Adhelm's Head, and sailing off Portland. The royal family returned two years later for a holiday and then returned every year until 1805.

In 1808 John Rainier (brother of the heroic Rear Admiral Peter Rainier, whose name was given to Mount Rainier near Seattle) arranged for a symbol of the town's undying loyalty and gratitude to be carved into the chalk downs above Osmington. And so an elegant silhouette of the King on horseback was created, around 324ft (99m) high, riding away from the town – presumably in a much healthier condition after his vacation. Once clearly visible from Weymouth, Portland and ships out at sea, today the chalk figure is weathered and

Stone-cut cottages beside the River Jordan in Sutton Poyntz

| 2h00 | 4 MILES | 6.4 KM | LEVEL 1 2 3 |

MAP: OS Explorer OL 15 Purbeck & South Dorset

START/FINISH: Church Lane in Osmington, just off the A353; grid ref: SY 724829

PATHS: farm and village lanes, woodland paths, field paths, 8 stiles

LANDSCAPE: sheltered green valley behind coastline and chalky ridge of White Horse Hill

PUBLIC TOILETS: none on route

TOURIST INFORMATION: Weymouth, tel: 01305 785747

THE PUB: The Springhead, Sutton Poyntz

🛈 One steady downland climb

Getting to the start

Osmington village is located north of the A353, 4 miles (6.4km) north of Weymouth. Limited roadside parking by the church.

Researched and written by:
David Hancock, Ann F Stonehouse

grey, but you can still pick out the graceful lines of the horse's legs and tail, and the King's distinctive cocked hat.

the walk

1 From Osmington church walk down the village street of pretty thatched cottages. At the junction keep on down **Church Lane**. Opposite **The Cartshed**, at the end of a wall, look carefully for and turn left up a long, steep flight of steps, signed **'Sutton Poyntz'**. The path rises through woodland. After a second set of steps bear right on the path which undulates through the trees. Cross a stile and continue straight on to the end of a field.

2 Cross a stile and turn immediately right to cross a second stile and walk down the field. Turn left through a gate and head straight across the field. Cross a **farm track**

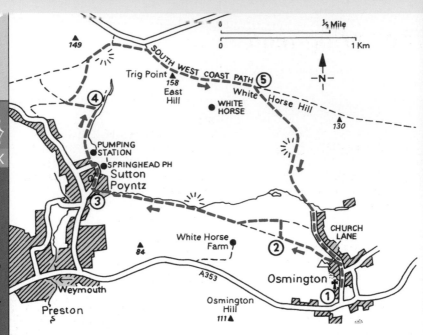

and bear ahead and right. Cross a pair of stiles and continue along the bottom of the field, looking to your right to see the **White Horse**. Continue though a gap. At the end of the next field bear left, through a gateway, then go straight on (**yellow marker**), towards Sutton Poyntz. Soon veer right, cross a **stream** and bear left by a gate. Follow the path to a stile and continue to the road.

3 Turn right, pass the **Mill House** and the tall, red brick mill on the left. Pass the **village pond** and **The Springhead** pub on the right. Bear left and right up a lane by

Springfield Cottage. Go through a gate and follow the track straight ahead. Cross a stile by another gate, with a **pumping station** on the right, below the bottom of the steep combe where the spring emerges.

4 Cross a stile by a gate and turn left up the **grassy lane**. About half-way up the hill turn right, up a track (the upper of two) that leads to the top above the combe, with great views along the valley and down to Weymouth Bay and Portland. Keep right on the green track, go through a gate and keep left along the field edge. Follow the path round to the right and walk up the field (a lane soon joins from the left). Stay on this track past the **trig point**. Go through a gate and keep straight on, with a good view to strip lynchets on the hillside ahead.

5 Go through a gate and bear down to the right, signed **'Osmington'**. The track leads down the hill, through a gate – look back to see the White Horse again. Follow the lane back up through the village to your car.

what to look for

As you walk along White Horse Hill there is a clear view of terracing on the grassy slopes of the combe ahead. These are strip lynchets, relics of a farming system introduced in the 12th and 13th centuries in Dorset, to maximise the land available for cultivation.

The Springhead

about the pub

The Springhead
Sutton Poyntz, Weymouth
Dorset DT3 6LW
Tel: 01305 832117

DIRECTIONS: in the centre of the village, which is signed off the A353 north east of Weymouth	
PARKING: 30	
OPEN: daily, all day in summer	
FOOD: no food Sunday evening	
BREWERY/COMPANY: free house	
REAL ALE: Flowers IPA, Greene King Old Speckled Hen	
DOGS: welcome in the bar	

The Victorian stone pub takes its name from the nearby spring and waterworks, which actually incorporates one of the funnels from Brunel's steamship, the Great Eastern. It stands in a grand location in a sleepy village beside the duck-pond and enjoys splendid views of the Dorset Downs – it's hard to imagine you are so close to bustling Weymouth. It is much modernised inside, and the open-plan carpeted bar and dining room have leather sofas and armchairs in cosy nooks and crannies, and old photos of the pub and village adorn the walls. The pub fairly buzzes on summer weekends, when the garden fills with families and the shady front benches that overlook the village pond and stream become much sought after, so arrive early on sunny days.

Food
The seasonal lunch menu takes in home-made soups, chicken liver parfait, baked chicken supreme, Thai vegetable curry, Caesar salad, and freshly battered fish and chips. Additional dishes may include rack of lamb, lemon sole and Lyme Bay plaice. Separate evening menu.

Family facilities
Families are made very welcome. Children are allowed inside and there's a play area at the far end of the garden.

☛ Where to go from here
The seaside resort of Weymouth has a number of good family attractions, including the Sea Life Park in Lodmoor Country Park, and the Deep Sea Adventure Centre, which tells of underwater exploration, shipwrecks and harbour life, with play areas for all ages (www.deepsea-adventure.co.uk).

A lost village at Higher Melcombe

A hilly circuit of farmland where, in centuries past, labour economics determined the pattern of a settlement.

Of Binghams and Melcomes

Be prepared for confusion. This walk passes Higher Melcombe, through Melcombe Bingham to Bingham's Melcombe, which is also known as Melcombe Horsey. And Melcombe Horsey was the name of a village at Higher Melcombe that has disappeared. Clear?

There has been a church at Bingham's Melcombe since before 1302. The current one dates from the 14th century. The church is cruciform in shape, two side chapels forming the arms of the cross. The Bingham chapel has a touching memorial to Thomas, infant son of Richard and Philadelphia Bingham, who died in 1711.

The Binghams were one of Dorset's leading Parliamentary families during the Civil War, and their mansion and gardens (not open to the public), of which you can only catch a glimpse, are magnificent. The Dower House, opposite the church, has fine octagonal window panes. By contrast, Higher Melcombe is, today, a solitary farm, set in a fertile green basin. The buildings are dominated by the old manor house,

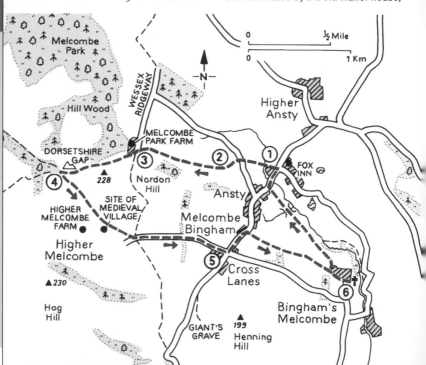

2h00 · **5 MILES** · **8 KM** · **LEVEL 1 2 3**

Above right: Blackmoor Vale

built in the mid-15th century for Sir John Horsey, with a chapel attached later. A village called Melcombe Horsey once occupied this lovely spot. According to the map the village simply disappeared in medieval times, but why?

The answer lies at Dorset's other Melcombe, the port of Melcombe Regis, now absorbed into Weymouth. Melcombe Regis has an unfortunate claim to fame for, in June 1348, the first case in Britain of bubonic plague – the Black Death – was brought ashore here. The disease spread through the county with devastating speed, wiping out between one third and one half of the population.

The feudal system that had operated until this time in Dorset, with labourers tied to manorial land, could not survive such losses and labour became a prime commodity. Workers moved to where they could be paid for their work as free men. Once-thriving villages like Melcombe Horsey were reduced to little hamlets, or sometimes a single isolated farm. The changes meant a severe reduction in arable cultivation, as prime farmland reverted to more manageable grazing.

the walk

1 Turn up the road and go immediately left across a stile and down a **waymarked path**. Cross a stile, bear right down the edge of the field and cross a stile at the bottom. Continue straight up the next field, cross a stile and road to go through a gate. Keep straight on to reach a **pair of stiles** in a hedge.

MAP: OS Explorer 117 Cerne Abbas & Bere Regis
START/FINISH: parking area on north side of village hall, Ansty; grid ref: ST 765031
PATHS: farmland, woodland tracks, ancient bridleway, road, 11 stiles
LANDSCAPE: gently rolling farmland, little lumpy hills, village
PUBLIC TOILETS: none on route
TOURIST INFORMATION: Blandford Forum, tel: 01258 454770
THE PUB: The Fox Inn, Lower Ansty
Care needed on stretch of road into Melcombe Bingham

Getting to the start
From the A35 north of Dorchester at the junction with A354 Blandford road, take the B3142, then first right for Cheselbourne and continue for 4 miles (6.4km) to Lower Ansty. The village hall and parking area are on the left, just before you reach The Fox Inn.

Researched and written by:
David Hancock, Ann F Stonehouse

The route passes the church at Bingham's Melcombe

2 Go across these stiles then bear right, across the field. Descend and go right, through a gate in the corner. Follow the **track** beside a hedge, then go through a gate and bend to the left.

3 Go into the farm and turn immediately left through the furthest of three gates, signposted **'Wessex Ridgeway'**. Walk along the edge of the field, above a wood. Go through a gate and continue straight ahead along the top of the ridge, enjoying superb views over the **Blackmoor Vale**. The track descends abruptly. Turn right, through a gate, to a crossroads of tracks at the **Dorsetshire Gap**.

4 Turn left down a bridleway through a deep cleft, signposted **'Higher**

Melcombe'**. Keep straight on through three fields. Ridges and hummocks in a field to your right are the only sign of the medieval village. Pass **Higher Melcombe Farm**, then go through a gate and turn left, on to a minor road, and walk beside an avenue of trees. Descend past some **houses** to a junction.

5 Turn left and walk on the road into **Melcombe Bingham**. Pass a row of houses, then turn right. Go through a gate to take the path straight ahead across the field. Pass the end of a strip of **woodland** and maintain your direction up the fence. Cross the stile at the top. Continue ahead through the trees and down the field towards **Bingham's Melcombe**. Cross a stile and turn right. Follow the drive round and down to the church.

6 Retrace your route to the stile and keep straight on past, up the field. Before the end turn left through a gate and bear right along a path. Where this divides keep left. Cross a stile and bear right along the field edge to a gate and descend on a track. Go straight ahead to cross a **footbridge**. Keep straight on, bear right over a stile in the fence and continue down the field. Just past some **bulging trees** turn left over a stile. Keep straight ahead then cross a stile on to the road. Turn right to return to your car.

what to look for

Ansty's handsome, flint-and-brick village hall is called the Old Brewery Hall. It was the original brewery for Hall and Woodhouse beer, made since 1777. The brewery's early success was founded on a government contract to supply ale to Dorsetshire troops awaiting an invasion by Napoleon that never came. Hall and Woodhouse moved to Blandford St Mary in 1899 and still thrive there today under their better-known Badger trademark.

The Fox Inn

about the pub

The Fox Inn
Lower Ansty, Blandford Forum
Dorset DT2 7PN
Tel: 01258 880328
www.foxansty.co.uk

DIRECTIONS: on the north edge of the village

PARKING: 40

OPEN: daily, all day

FOOD: daily

BREWERY/COMPANY: Hall and Woodhouse Brewery

REAL ALE: Badger Best, Tanglefoot and seasonal ale

DOGS: welcome in the bar

ROOMS: 12 en suite

Deep in Thomas Hardy territory, lost in narrow country lanes, this reassuringly civilised brick-and-flint pub was built 250 years ago as Broadclose. It was the home of Charles Hall, founder of the Ansty Brewery (later to become Hall and Woodhouse, which now owns the pub). It has been sympathetically refurbished by the brewery in keeping with the style and history of the property. You'll find a wealth of oak panelling in the Woodhouse Restaurant, while the informal lounge bar has upholstered wall bench seating, and old family photographs decorate the walls. Upstairs, the bedrooms mostly enjoy country views. There's a grassed area to the front with picnic benches, and a swimming pool to the rear for residents' use.

Food

Varied menus are served here. Choices range from patés and soups for starters to rack of lamb, pork and ale sausages with mash and onion gravy, and beef Wellington in the restaurant, to home made pies, lasagne, ham, egg and chips and chicken risotto on the bar menu. Snacks include ploughman's lunches. Sunday carvery roasts.

Family facilities

Children of all ages are welcome in the pub. High chairs are available and youngsters have their own menu to select from.

☛ Where to go from here

Athelhampton House, south of here and off the A35 near Puddletown, is one of England's most majestic old mansions, stuffed with treasures, and with parts dating back to 1485 (www.athelhampton.co.uk).

Durdle Door and Lulworth Cove

An exhilarating walk on a spectacular piece of coastline.

Lulworth Cove

Lulworth Cove is an almost perfectly circular bay on Dorset's southern coast. Its pristine condition and geological importance earned it World Heritage status in 2002. The cove provides a secure anchorage for small fishing boats and pleasure craft, and a sun-trap of safe water for summer bathers. The cliffs around the eastern side of the bay are crumbly soft and brightly coloured in some places. The geology is intriguing and a visit to the Heritage Centre will help you to sort it out.

The oldest layer, easily identified here, is the gleaming white Portland stone. It is a fine-grained oolite, around 140 million years old. It consists of tightly compressed, fossilised shells – the flat-coiled ones are ammonites. Occasional giant ammonites, called titanites, may be seen incorporated into house walls across Purbeck. Like the rock of Bat's Head, it may contain speckled bands of flinty chert. Above this is a layer of Purbeck marble, a limestone rich in the fossils of vertebrates. This is where dinosaur fish and reptile fossils are usually found. The soft layer above this consists of Wealden beds, a belt of colourful clays, silts and sands, that are unstable and prone to landslips when exposed. Crumbly, white chalk overlays the Wealden beds. The chalk consists of the remains of microscopic sea creatures and shells deposited over a long

Durdle Door on the Lulworth coast

what to look for

Don't miss the baby-blue painted Dolls House on the way down to the harbour in Lulworth Cove. It's a fisherman's cottage dating from 1861. You may find it difficult to believe that 11 children were raised in this tiny house. Contrast its cramped simplicity with the dwelling opposite, with diamond-pane windows and a cosy thatched roof, built in a decorative style known as 'cottage orné'.

Boats moored in the bay at West Lulworth

period of time when a deep sea covered much of Dorset, some 75 million years ago.

This is the chalk that underlies Dorset's famous downland and is seen in the exposed soft, eroded cliffs at White Nothe. Hard nodules and bands of flint appear in the chalk – it's a purer type of chert – and in its gravel beach form it protects long stretches of this fragile coast.

the walk

1 From the corner of the car park at Durdle Door Caravan Park take the path down to **Durdle Door**. Return the same way but before steeply ascending fork right, signed to **Lulworth Cove**. Follow the path along the coast and down to the cove (the Heritage Centre and Stair Hole on the right are worth visiting).

2 Turn sharp left up steps, signed to **Bindon Hill**. Walk through a wooded area to a stile, then turn sharp right to skirt the rim of the cove. Near the top take the path left to Bindon Hill and on the brow, at a junction with a wider path, turn right. Walk across **ancient earthworks** and by the entrance to **Lulworth Army Ranges**, then turn left down towards the village of **West Lulworth**. Cross a stile and bear half-left across a field, crossing the stile on the left just before the bottom.

3 Continue along a fenced path at the back of the village. The path swings left up some **steps** (steps right lead down to the Main Street where you turn right for the

2h00 **3.25 MILES** **5.3 KM** **LEVEL 1 2 3**

MAP: OS Explorer OL 15 Purbeck & South Dorset

START/FINISH: car park (fee) above Durdle Door; grid ref: SY 811804

PATHS: stone path, grassy tracks, tarmac, 8 stiles

LANDSCAPE: steeply rolling cliffs beside sea, green inland

PUBLIC TOILETS: by Heritage Centre in Lulworth, and just above Lulworth Cove

TOURIST INFORMATION: Weymouth, tel: 01305 785747

THE PUB: The Castle Inn, West Lulworth

🛈 Take heed of warning signs – steep paths (up and down) and cliff edges. A short walk but really for fitter, older children.

Getting to the start

From the A352 west of Wareham take the B3070 south for East Lulworth and continue to West Lulworth. Pass the Castle Inn and turn first right, passing the church. In 0.75 mile (1.2km) turn left, down past Durdle Door Caravan Park, to the car park.

Researched and written by:
Ann F Stonehouse, Peter Toms

Castle Inn), then along to an unmade road. At the junction with **Bindon Road** turn left, and in 25yds (23m) turn right over a stile, signed to Lulworth Cove. In 10yds (9m) fork right through a **gate** and keep to the right edge of the field. At the **waymarker**, turn right over a stile, signed Durdle Door. Descend the fenced path to the road.

4 Turn right, and in 50yds (46m) turn left to **Durdle Door**. Cross the stile and walk along the left hand edge of a field. After the next stile ascend steps through a small wood to a stile and turn right along a chalk path, signed to **Durdle Door Camp Site**. Ignore the parallel track, and continue across fields. After four stiles return to the corner of the car park.

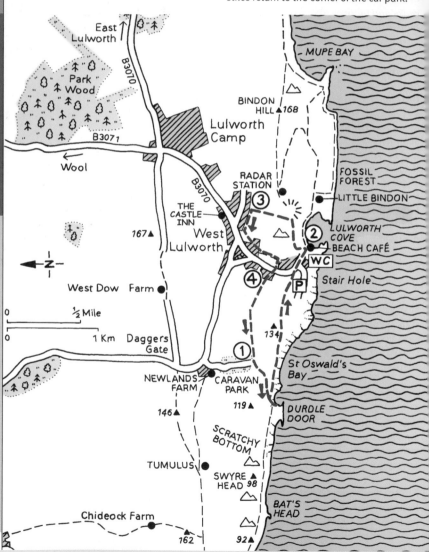

The Castle Inn

This is a picturesque thatched and beamed inn, hidden away in a lovely spot near Lulworth Cove, close to great coastal walks and popular attractions. It was built in the 17th century, and is named after a castle that once existed near by. It was originally called the Jolly Sailor, before being destroyed by fire in 1929. Restoration over the years has resulted in two main bars, one with flagstones and an open fire, and a cosy, more modern lounge and dining room. The draw in summer among the hordes of visitors that flock to this beautiful coastline are the prize-winning terraced gardens. These are packed with plants, garden furniture, a water feature, barbecue, boules pitch and giant chess board. Comfortable, well-equipped bedrooms are tucked beneath the heavy thatch.

is open all year and serves a multitude of fresh, locally caught fish.

Where to go from here

Lulworth Castle is set in glorious parkland, just inland at East Lulworth (www.lulworth.com). It has a restored kitchen, and there are great views from the top of its tower. You'll also find an animal farm for children, an indoor activity room and pitch and putt to enjoy in the grounds.

Food

The wide-ranging menu offers a choice of some 50 dishes, from chicken and ham pie, sirloin steak, or liver and bacon and seafood stew, to exotic cuts like crocodile, ostrich or kangaroo, plus a variety of flambé dishes cooked at the table. Lighter lunchtime snacks and Sunday roast lunches.

Family facilities

Children are welcome inside the pub. High chairs, baby-changing facilities, small portions, children's menu and small cutlery are all available. There's plenty to keep children amused in the garden.

Alternative refreshment stops

In Lulworth the Heritage Centre café includes family meals and baguettes. Just down the hill, the Lulworth Cove Hotel

about the pub

The Castle Inn
West Lulworth, Wareham
Dorset BH20 5RN
Tel: 01929 400311
www.thecastleinn-lulworthcove.co.uk

DIRECTIONS: on the main street	
PARKING: 20	
OPEN: daily	
FOOD: daily	
BREWERY/COMPANY: free house	
REAL ALE: Ringwood Best, Gales HSB	
DOGS: welcome in the bar	
ROOMS: 11 en suite	

Corfe Castle circuit

WALK

A loop to Kingston from
a romantic ruined castle.

Corfe Castle

DORSET

A castle condemned

The huge and toothy ruin of Corfe Castle
seems to fill the gap in the wall of the
Purbeck Hills. It stands on a high mound, and
must have been massively imposing when
whole. The castle has a grim history. In AD 978
a youthful King Edward was murdered here
while visiting his stepmother. His body was
buried without ceremony at Wareham, while
his half-brother took the throne as Ethelred
II. However, stories of miracles resulted in
Edward's body being exhumed and
transported to Shaftesbury, where an
abbey grew up in his honour.

The Normans realised the commanding
role a castle could play in defence at Corfe. In
around 1106, the big square keep was built.
King John used it as a lifelong prison for his
niece Eleanor, a potential threat to his
throne. The unfortunate Edward II, deposed
by his wife Isabella and Roger de Mortimer,
was also imprisoned here briefly. The castle
again came to the fore during the Civil War.
Its owner, Sir John Bankes sided with the
King. However, it was his spirited wife Mary
who was left, with a handful of women and
just five men, to fight off a siege in 1642.

It is said that the Roundheads took the
lead from the church roof to make their
bullets, and stored their powder and shot
in the organ pipes. Despite reinforcements,
they failed to take the castle. After a second,
more sustained siege, the castle was
betrayed in 1646 by one of its defenders
and Lady Bankes was forced to give it up.
The castle was deliberately destroyed, to
prevent its further use.

the walk

1 From the car park bear right then right
again on to **West Street**. At the end, go
straight on over a cattle grid. Bear left on
a path across the heath, the line being
Kingston church tower. Cross duckboards
and go uphill, forking right by a **tumulus**,
and walk to the right of a stone block.
Continue over the brow of the hill and
descend in line with the church tower. The
path gradually veers right and leaves the
Common by way of a kissing gate, stiles and
footbridges.

2 Bear half-left across a field, and across
the next, regaining the line of the tower.
Go over a **bridge** and ascend a wooded
path. Cross a stile and continue up the left
edge of a field. Maintain direction after the
next stile. Go through a thick hedge and
head straight across the next field (the **flag
pole** on the church tower being the line) to
a kissing gate and turn right up a track. On
the ascent fork left, taking the path up
through the **woods**.

3 At the top, turn left to the road and
walk down through the village. At the
junction by the **Scott Arms** turn right. After
the **converted church**, go over a stile on
the left and bear half-right, signposted
to **Afflington**. Pass through a gate at the
bottom corner of the field and continue
along the left boundary of the next field to
a stile in the corner. Shortly, bear left down
through scrubland, then turn left on to a
stony track. As this bears right take the
path left (**Purbeck Way**) over a stile and go
down the track left into a field.

2h00 · **4.25 MILES** · **6.8 KM** · **LEVEL 1 2 3**

4 Turn right, go through a **gate** and soon go right over a stile. Cross a narrow wooded strip to a stile and turn left beside the woods. Go over a further stile and proceed straight on, soon to bear left through a gate and around the left edge of a field. Turn left over a stile and **footbridge**, then another stile and turn sharp right. Cross a metalled drive, a stile, a causeway and bridge on to the **Common**.

5 Go straight on over Corfe Common towards the **castle**. Bear left at a **concrete marker**, and go right to a gate. Cross the B3069, go through a gate and straight on, later bearing right behind **houses**. Go through a kissing gate and follow the path (still signed Purbeck Way) towards the centre of Corfe. After it winds through housing go across fields into a **playground**. Turn left then right into West Street to reach the **square**.

The ruins of Corfe Castle, a stronghold which was destroyed during the Civil War

MAP: OS Explorer OL 15 Purbeck & South Dorset
START/FINISH: Corfe Castle; village pay car park; grid ref: SY 958818
PATHS: village lanes, rocky lanes (slippery after rain), moorland tracks, grassy paths
LANDSCAPE: downland, heathland, village streets
PUBLIC TOILETS: car park, Corfe Castle
TOURIST INFORMATION: Wareham, tel: 01929 552740
THE PUB: The Greyhound Inn, Corfe Castle
❶ The main A351 through Corfe is often busy and dangerous.

Getting to the start

The small township of Corfe Castle stands on the A351, midway between Wareham and Swanage, 5 miles (8km) south east of Wareham. The car park is off West Street, close to the village centre.

Researched and written by:
Ann F Stonehouse, Peter Toms

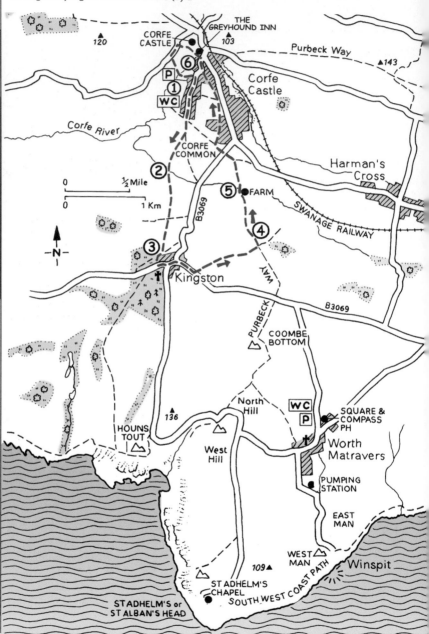

6 Turn left by the castle on the path below the **walls**. Go left up the road and soon left again by a gate and over a stile (by a sign to **The Rings**). Cross the fields via series of gates to return to the car park.

THE GREYHOUND INN

CORFE CASTLE

▲120

▲103

Purbeck Way

▲143

P

①

⑥

Corfe Castle

WC

Corfe River

CORFE COMMON

Harman's Cross

②

0   ½ Mile

0   1 Km

⑤ FARM

B3069

SWANAGE RAILWAY

④

−N−

③

Kingston

PURBECK WAY

B3069

COOMBE BOTTOM

North Hill

WC

P

SQUARE & COMPASS PH

▲136

Worth Matravers

HOUNS TOUT

West Hill

PUMPING STATION

EAST MAN

109▲

WEST MAN

Winspit

ST ADHELM'S CHAPEL

SOUTH WEST COAST PATH

ST ADHELM'S or ST ALBAN'S HEAD

The Greyhound Inn

The battlements of Corfe Castle, once one of England's five royal castles, not only form the dramatic backdrop, but probably furnished the stones to build the Greyhound – originally two cottages with stables – in the 16th century. The pub's garden borders the moat of the castle, and there over super views of the Purbeck Hills, making it a popular place to retreat to after this walk, or following a stroll around the castle ruins. Inside, three pleasant and small low-beamed areas off the main bar have oak panelling, lots of paintings, brass artefacts, and old photos of the village and castle. If you're lucky your visit may coincide with one of Greyhound's three annual beer festivals, when you can join in the fun of sampling 50 real ales and tucking in to the giant hog roast in the garden.

Food

In addition to the weekend carvery and a deli bar where you can create your own sandwich, the regular menu lists soups, salads, ploughman's lunches, farmhouse chicken pie, and beefburgers. Try the chargrilled meat baskets, or order fresh fish or seafood from the daily chalkboard, perhaps whole sea bass, cold lobster salad or monkfish medallions.

Family facilities

Children will love it here. There's a cosy family room kitted out with toys and games, a children's menu, high chairs for youngsters, baby food can be warmed up, and the garden is safe to play in.

Alternative refreshment stops

At the half-way point in Kingston you will find the Scott Arms. There's also a good range of pubs and tea rooms in Corfe Castle.

☞ Where to go from here

Catch the steam train to the coastal resort of Swanage, for the Studland Heritage Centre, the restored Victorian Pier, amusements and the sandy beach (www.swanagerailway.co.uk).

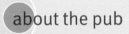

about the pub

The Greyhound Inn

The Square, Corfe Castle
Wareham, Dorset BH20 5EZ
Tel: 01929 480205

DIRECTIONS: in the centre of Corfe Castle
PARKING: use car park on West Street
OPEN: daily, all day in summer, and all day Saturday and Sunday in winter
FOOD: daily, all day in summer
BREWERY/COMPANY: Enterprise Inns
REAL ALE: Ringwood Fortyniner, Gales Best, Hampshire Bohemian Rhapsody
DOGS: welcome indoors

Around the Moors Valley Country Park

Moors Valley

HAMPSHIRE

Exploring woodland and lakes, with extra loops to create your own route.

A miniature railway

The tracks may only be 7.25 inches (18.5cm) wide, but there's a real railway atmosphere to the miniature line at the Moors Valley Country Park. Its steam locomotives, carriages and goods vans thread their way around a landscaped loop beside the Moors Lake, and the 1-mile (1.6km) circuit is complete with a station, signal box and four tunnels.

The Moors Lake itself was built as a 'safety valve' to contain flooding in the area, which is liable after heavy rainfall. Some of the spoil from the lake was used to landscape the golf course and these developments provided the inspiration for the 1,500-acre (608ha) country park.

Work on the miniature railway began in 1985 as tracks were laid out and Kingsmere station was created from former farm buildings on the site. Many of the locomotives, rolling stock and carriages were brought from the Tucktonia Leisure Centre at Christchurch, and the new line opened to the public in July 1986. The railway is popular with both adults and children, and the ten-minute ride takes you past the main signal box and along the banks of the lake before looping around the play area on the way back to Kingsmere station. The railway is open daily from late May to early September, as well as during Easter and the Christmas holidays.

the ride

1 Leave the car park by the road entrance, zig-zag across **Hurn Lane** and join the combined cycleway/pavement under the A31. Bear left past the **phone-box**, then stop at the A31 slip road. Cross with care, then bear left on to the **Castleman Trail** towards Ashley Heath. The narrow gravel track bears to the right and pulls clear of the A31 through a tunnel of **young oak trees**. Soon the old line widens out into a 'dual carriageway' of narrow tracks separated by gorse and brambles. Watch out for cars as you cross the lane at **Holly Grove Farm**. You'll speed along the next

A packed model railway ride through Moors Valley Country Park

section to the road crossing at **Ashley Heath**. Stop here, and cross **Horton Road** with care. There's a convenience shop on your right as you rejoin the Castleman Trail and continue along the tree-shaded **cycleway**. Very soon, pass a section of the **former platform** at Ashley Heath, complete with its railway name-board. Continue for 600yds (549m), then look out for the narrow exit into **Forest Edge Drive** on the right.

2 Go through here and follow this residential road to the T-junction with Horton Road. Take care as you zig-zag left and right into the **Moors Valley Country Park** – it's only 50yds (46m), but you may prefer to wheel your bike along the pavement beside this busy road. Follow the tarred entrance road for the last 0.5 mile (800m) to reach the **visitor centre**, with a restaurant, toilets and other facilities. For the shortest ride, turn here and retrace the outward route back to the start. But it's well worth extending your visit by picking up a park map and following one of the four waymarked cycle routes around the forest.

3 The **Corsican Circuit** (2 miles/3.2km) is the basic ring at the heart of the park, which you can extend by adding one or more of the loops. It leads east from the visitor centre and loops anti-clockwise. The level route passes the **Play Trail entrance**, then circles back on good, gravelled forest rides.

4 Take the **Watchmoor Loop** (1.5 miles/ 2.3km) off the Corsican Circuit. It follows sandy tracks and penetrates some of the quieter areas of the forest. You'll see areas of open heathland, as well as plenty of light conifer woodland where the smell of the

---

| 2h00 | 12 MILES | 19.3 KM | LEVEL 2 |

SHORTER ALTERNATIVE ROUTE

| 1h00 | 5.5 MILES | 8.8 KM | LEVEL 1 |

MAP: OS Explorer OL22 New Forest
START/FINISH: Ashley Twinning (free) car park; grid ref: SU 139048
TRAILS/TRACKS: old railway cycleway, roads and forest tracks
LANDSCAPE: the tree-lined old railway leads into mixed woodland, heath and lakes
PUBLIC TOILETS: Moors Valley Country Park
TOURIST INFORMATION: Ringwood, tel: 01425 470896
CYCLE HIRE: Moors Valley Country Park visitor centre, tel: 01425 470721
THE PUB: The Old Beams, Ibsley
🔵 Two main road crossings and slow-moving traffic on country park access road. Suitability: inexperienced riders and children over 7 depending on trail option selected.

Getting to the start
The car park is 0.5 miles (800m) south west of Ringwood off the A31. Leave the A31 at the B3081 junction, then take the Hurn Lane exit from the junction roundabout for the car park.

Why do this cycle ride?
A versatile route: at its simplest, you'll follow a level, traffic-free cycleway to the Moors Valley Country Park, with its superb range of family-friendly facilities and attractions. You can extend or vary this basic route by following one or more of the traffic-free cycle trails within the park.

Researched and written by: David Foster

8

🚲
CYCLE

Moors Valley

HAMPSHIRE

pines mixes with the sweet scent of bracken, before rejoining the Corsican Circuit.

5 At this point you can also detour off on the **Somerley Loop** (1 mile/1.6km). This weaves its way over gravel and dirt tracks through some of the denser parts of the forest, though there are still some wide heather verges in places. It is the most undulating of the park trails, with a steep downhill section near the end.

6 The Somerley Loop joins on to the **Crane Loop** (2 miles/3.2km), which on its own is great for young families. This pretty route heads out beside the **golf course** and **Crane Lake**, before returning beside the miniature railway. You'll mainly follow tarred trails, though there are some gravel and dirt sections, too. Watch out for cars on the final section, which shares one of the park roads.

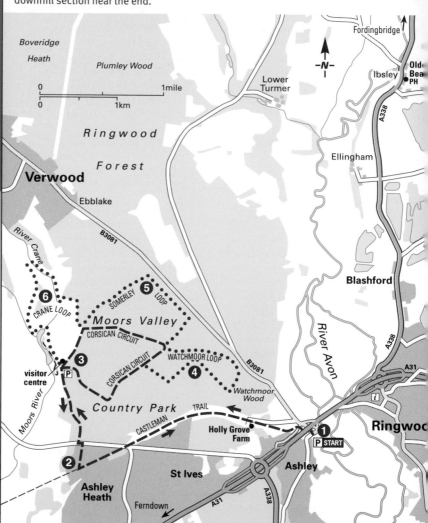

The Old Beams

The exterior of this 600-year-old cruck-beamed cottage is everything you would expect of an untouched country pub. The roof is neatly thatched, the walls are half-timbered and the building is flanked by an orchard garden. But all is not what it seems. Venturing inside is like entering Dr Who's Tardis, and beyond the pretty façade you will find a vast open-plan area, with a conservatory-style extension dominated by a central hooded fireplace. Furnishings range from dark wood tables and chairs to pine farmhouse tables. Along one side is the grand buffet table, laden with cold meats, seafood and fresh salads, drawing diners all day long.

Food

In addition to the usual sandwiches and ploughman's, there's a buffet counter displaying a wide range of cold meats and

about the pub

The Old Beams
Salisbury Road, Ibsley
Ringwood, Hampshire BH24 3PP
Tel: 01425 473387

DIRECTIONS: beside the A338 Ringwood-to-Salisbury road, 3 miles (4.8km) north of Ringwood
PARKING: 100
OPEN: daily, all day
FOOD: daily, all day
BREWERY/COMPANY: Greene King Brewery
REAL ALE: Greene King IPA & Abbot Ale, Ringwood Best

salads. Hot dishes include steak and ale pie, fish and chips, lamb slow cooked with rosemary and red wine on thyme mash, mixed grill and chargrilled tuna with white wine and coriander sauce. Sunday roast carvery lunches are served all afternoon.

Family facilities

Expect a genuine welcome, with smaller portions and standard children's menu available. There are also high chairs and baby-changing facilities.

Alternative refreshment stops

Seasons Restaurant at Moors Valley Country Park serves breakfast, lunches and afternoon teas.

☛ Where to go from here

At the Dorset Heavy Horse Centre near Verwood you'll see magnificent Shire horses, meet and groom donkeys and miniature Shetland ponies, and help feed the many animals at the centre, including Lulu the llama. Café, picnic and play areas (www.dorset-heavy-horse-centre.co.uk).

A circuit around Linwood

Venture off the beaten track and mix with wildlife in the heart of the New Forest.

New Forest deer

You'll often see deer along this trail, especially early in the morning or around dusk – go quietly for the best chance of seeing these timid woodland residents in their natural habitat. Keep an eye out for roe deer in the cultivated fields close to Dockens Water, between the start of the ride and the point where you join the tarred lane leading up to the Red Shoot Inn. These graceful creatures are 24–28 inches

(61–71cm) high at the shoulder and the males have short, forked antlers. Roe deer have rich reddish-brown coats from May to September, but turn greyer in winter and develop a white patch on the rump.

You'll occasionally spot red deer in the same area, especially on the open heath near Black Barrow. These are our largest native species, and a fully-grown male with his splendid russet coat and impressive antlers may stand nearly 4ft (1.2m) tall at the shoulder. The males are at their boldest when competing for females during the mating season in early autumn.

Fallow deer may pop up almost anywhere on the ride, but a favourite haunt

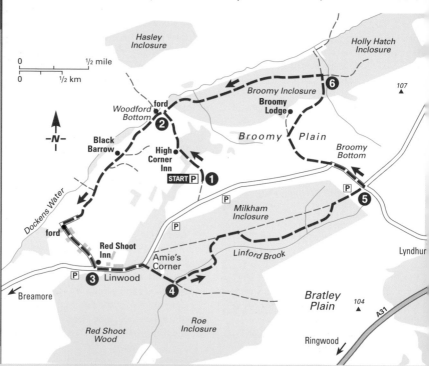

is in Broomy Bottom, off to your right as you cross Broomy Plain. With their reddish-fawn coats dappled with white spots, these appealing animals have white rumps and a black line running up the tail. The males have broad antlers and stand up to 3ft (0.9m) tall at the shoulder.

the ride

1 Turn right out of the car park and pass the end of the gravel track which leads up to the **High Corner Inn**.

2 At Woodford Bottom bear left at the wooden barrier on your right and pass the ford across the Dockens Water stream, also on your right. Keep to the waymarked cycle route as it follows the gravelled track that winds across the open heath, past a few scattered houses and the tree-capped mound of **Black Barrow**. A few smaller tracks lead off to left and right, but the main gravelled trail is easy enough to follow. Keep straight on as a similar track leads in from your left near the thatched Bogmyrtle Cottage, until you join a tarred lane. Almost at once the lane turns sharp left through a tiny ford and climbs gently up to the road junction at the **Red Shoot Inn**.

3 Turn left opposite the post-box, still following the waymarked cycle route, and continue to climb until the road levels off and swings to the left at **Amie's Corner**. Fork right here, sticking with the waymarked cycle route as it joins a gravelled forest track. The trail dives into Milkham Inclosure through wooden gates beside an attractive whitewashed cottage, then drops to a bridge over the Linford Brook.

1h45 · 7 MILES · 11.3 KM · LEVEL 2

MAP: OS Explorer OL22 New Forest
START/FINISH: Spring Bushes car park, Linwood; grid ref: SU 196107
TRAILS/TRACKS: gravelled forest tracks, two short sections on rural lanes
LANDSCAPE: broadleaf and coniferous woodland interspersed with open heathland
PUBLIC TOILETS: none on route
TOURIST INFORMATION: Lyndhurst, tel: 023 8028 2269
CYCLE HIRE: Country Lanes, 9 Shaftesbury Street, Fordingbridge, tel: 01425 655022
THE PUB: The High Corner Inn, Linwood
⓵ Moderate hills, some uneven and stony tracks. Suitable for older children, off-road riding experience useful.

Getting to the start

Linwood is a village on a minor road north east of Ringwood. Spring Bushes car park is on the road that runs west from Emery Down, near Lyndhurst, to Rockford, just north of Ringwood.

Why do this cycle ride?

This relatively remote ride offers peace and quiet, and the opportunity to see the New Forest at its best. You'll follow waymarked Forestry Commission off-road cycle tracks deep into the heart of the Forest, with two short sections on tarred roads where you will need to watch out for the occasional car. There are plenty of opportunities for birdwatching or studying the other wildlife.

Researched and written by: David Foster

A family cycles through the countryside at Linwood

4 A few yards further on turn left at the numbered waymark post 5, then follow the track as it winds through open mixed woodland and re-crosses the **Linford Brook**. Continue as the track bears right at the next **waymark post**, then right again in front of a pair of wooden gates where you enter an area of mainly coniferous woodland. A pair of wooden gates punctuates your progress to the top of the hill, where further gates lead you out into the Forestry Commission's **Milkham car park**. Go through here, cross the car park, and stop at the road junction.

5 Turn left towards **Linwood** and follow the narrow tarred lane for 500yds (457m) until it bears away to the left. Fork right here on to the waymarked cycle trail that follows the gravel track towards **Broomy Lodge** and **Holly Hatch**. Here your route crosses the high

heathland plateau of **Broomy Plain**. This is a good spot to see Dartford warblers, meadow pipits and stonechats, and you'll also enjoy long views towards Cranborne Chase and the Wiltshire Downs. Bear right at the next fork and follow the trail down into **Holly Hatch Inclosure**.

6 At the foot of the hill, numbered **waymark post 3** stands at the forest crossroads. Turn left here, on to a lovely tree-shaded track with soft green verges that leads you through the **oak woods**. Two pairs of wooden gates mark your progress through the inclosure, and at length the oaks give way to conifers. Follow the waymarked trail until you rejoin your outward route at a low wooden barrier. Turn left here, and climb the short hill back to the **High Corner Inn**.

The High Corner Inn

The High Corner is an early 18th-century inn, much extended and modernised. It is set in 7 acres (2.8ha) of the New Forest and hidden down an old drovers' track off a narrow Forest lane. A quiet hideaway in winter, mobbed in high summer due to its heart-of-the-Forest location, it is a popular retreat for families, offering numerous bar-free rooms, an outdoor adventure playground and miles of easy New Forest walks. Although extensively refurbished, this rambling old building retains a wealth of beams, wooden and flagstone floors, and a blazing winter log fire in the cosy main bar. There's a separate food servery, plus top-notch Wadworth ales on tap and overnight accommodation in eight well-equipped rooms.

Food

An extensive printed menu includes sandwiches, ploughman's lunches and salads, as well as freshly battered haddock and chips, beef and 6X pie and sizzling steak platters. Look to the blackboard for daily soups, daily roasts or the likes of baked trout with pine nuts and chargrilled pork loin with spiced apple cream.

Family facilities

This is a great family pub – there's a children's menu, family areas, high chairs and a woodland garden with adventure playground.

Alternative refreshment stops

Also owned by Wadworth Brewery, the Red Shoot Inn offers home-cooked meals and brews its own beer behind the pub.

about the pub

The High Corner Inn
Linwood, Ringwood
Hampshire BH24 3QY
Tel: 01425 473973

DIRECTIONS: a gravel track to the High Corner Inn branches off the road, 400yds (366m) west of the start point
PARKING: 200
OPEN: daily, all day in summer, and all day Sunday in winter
FOOD: daily, all day July and August
BREWERY/COMPANY: Wadworth Brewery
REAL ALE: Wadworth Henry's IPA, 6X and JCB
ROOMS: 7 en suite

☛ Where to go from here

Breamore House, north of here off the A338, is a handsome old manor house which dates back to 1583. It has a fine collection of paintings and china, and a countryside museum which includes steam engines (www.breamorehouse.com).

A New Forest loop from Burley

CYCLE

Burley

HAMPSHIRE

A varied ride from a popular village via 'Castleman's Corkscrew'.

The Castleman Trail

Railway interest is all around you on the mid-section of this ride, which reaches its climax at Holmsley's old station. The Castleman Trail follows the broad, level trackbed of the original main line to Dorchester. The railway was promoted by Charles Castleman, a Wimborne solicitor, who planned the line through his home town. This wasn't exactly the most direct route, and critics quickly dubbed it 'Castleman's Corkscrew'.

The railway opened in 1847, but was swallowed up by the larger and more powerful London & South Western Railway in the following year. At this time Bournemouth was little more than a sleepy village, but passengers for Christchurch could catch a linking coach service from Holmsley station, which was originally known as 'Christchurch Road'. After Bournemouth and Christchurch were linked to the national rail network, Holmsley's traffic evaporated. The station continued to serve its small local community, and handled timber from the nearby inclosures. Its rural seclusion was interrupted for a few years during the Second World War, when the little station became the gateway for a

above: The war memorial in Burley
below: An open path though woodland

...ew RAF airfield at Plain Heath. After the war, the railway fell victim to the growing popularity of road transport. Passenger traffic dwindled again and, in 1964, 'Castleman's Corkscrew' was finally axed in the notorious cuts made by Dr Beeching.

the ride

1 Turn right out of the car park, stop at the road junction, and continue straight ahead. Fork left at the **war memorial** into Pound Lane, signed to Bransgore. Pass the Forest Teahouse and cider shop, then follow the lane out over the heath to **Burbush Hill**.

2 Fork left just before the old railway bridge, following the waymarked off-road cycle track through the Forestry Commission's car park and down on to the **old railway line**. The Castleman Trail begins in a lovely sandy cutting, which is smothered with brilliant purple heather in late summer. Soon the old line emerges from the cutting onto a low embankment, with good views out over the boggy heath. You'll often see horse riders in the area and birdwatchers should look out for green woodpeckers, as well as for lapwings, curlews and redshanks, which nest on the heath in early summer. The trail rises briefly to the broken brickwork of **Greenberry Bridge**, which survived the closure of the

| 1h00 | 6 MILES | 9.7 KM | LEVEL 1 2 3 |

MAP: OS Explorer OL22 New Forest
START/FINISH: public fee-paying car park, Burley; grid ref: SU 211030
TRAILS/TRACKS: busy village centre, quiet lanes and an old railway route
LANDSCAPE: bare open heathland contrasts with pretty cottages and wooded village lanes
PUBLIC TOILETS: opposite car park, Burley
TOURIST INFORMATION: Lyndhurst, tel: 023 8028 2269
CYCLE HIRE: Forest Leisure Cycling, The Cross, Burley, tel: 01425 403584
THE PUB: The Queens Head, Burley
🛈 Burley's streets get busy at weekends and during holiday periods. Good traffic sense required.

Getting to the start

Burley village is on a minor road south east of Ringwood, between the A31 and the A35. Leave the A31 at Picket Post, 1 mile (1.6km) east of Ringwood, and follow the signposted route through Burley Street to Burley. Keep left at the war memorial in the centre of the village, and you'll find The Queens Head immediately on your left, with the public car park entrance just beyond the pub's own car park.

Why do this cycle ride?

This route takes you through the heart of the bustling New Forest village of Burley, with its antique shops, tea rooms and horse-drawn wagon rides. In complete contrast, the Castleman cycle trail is the perfect way to experience the surrounding heathland from a level stretch of old railway line. There are good opportunities for birdwatching, and you can visit the Old Station tea rooms at Holmsley.

Researched and written by: David Foster

Burley

HAMPSHIRE

CYCLE

railway, only to be demolished in 1995 when it became unsafe. Continue to the low **wooden barriers** that guard the minor road crossing at **Holmsley Passage**, where you can still see short sections of the original railway lines embedded in the road surface.

3 If you wish, you can shorten the ride by turning left here. To complete the full route, cross the road and continue along the **old railway line**. The trail becomes more shaded as it runs perfectly straight through an avenue of young oak trees. The track crosses **two small bridges** that herald the approach to Holmsley Station. Look out for the **old brick platform** on your right before dismounting at the wooden gate that marks the end of the cycle track.

4 Beyond the gate and across the road, the **Old Station tea rooms** are well worth a visit for morning coffee, home-

cooked lunches and cream teas. There's a pleasant garden, as well as a gift shop where you can buy a souvenir of your visit to this unusual refreshment stop. Turn here and retrace your outward route to **Holmsley Passage** (Point 3). Turn right on to the quiet lane, follow it up the hill and stop at the 5-way junction.

5 Cross straight over towards **Burley Lawn** and zig-zag left, then right, past the **White Buck Inn** into Bennetts Lane.

6 Bear left at the next junction into Beechwood Lane and keep straight on through **Lester Square** until you reach a T-junction. Turn left here towards Burley, and continue past the little brick-built **church** of St John the Baptist for the final 400yds (366m) back to the car park.

The Queens Head

Family facilities
Children are very welcome in the pub and there's a separate family area and children's menu. Youngsters will love to see the New Forest ponies that often congregate outside the pub.

Alternative refreshment stops
Tea rooms and the Burley Inn in Burley, the White Buck Inn at Burley Lawn, and the Old Station tea rooms at Holmsley are all good alternatives.

☛ Where to go from here
For more information about the New Forest area and its varied wildlife, visit the New Forest Museum and Visitor Centre in nearby Lyndhurst, with exhibitions and an audio-visual show (www.newforestmuseum.org.uk).

The Queen's Head was built in 1633, which makes it one of the oldest buildings in the New Forest. It became a smugglers' haunt in the 17th century, when contraband rum, brandy and tobacco was stored in the spacious cellars, well away from the coast. The main bar is named after Jack Warnes, an infamous local smuggler. The pub has been well modernised over the years and retains plenty of old timbers and panelling, wooden, flagstone and carpeted floors, and a fine Jacobean fireplace where a log fires blazes in winter. You'll find local beers from Ringwood Brewery on handpump and, for sunny summer days, a shaded courtyard garden with picnic tables.

Food
Food is traditional and the lunch and dinner menus are extensive. At lunch expect 'light bites' – seasonal soups, ploughman's and risotto, pasta, salads and sandwiches, alongside beer battered cod, steak and ale pie and specials such as lasagne and cottage pie. Dinner adds potted crab, rack of lamb, venison pie and roast duck with orange and shallot sauce. Sunday roast lunches.

about the pub

The Queens Head
The Cross, Burley
Ringwood, Hampshire BN24 4AB
Tel: 01425 403423

DIRECTIONS:	in the centre of the village
PARKING:	30
OPEN:	daily, all day
FOOD:	daily, all day
BREWERY/COMPANY:	Greene King
REAL ALE:	Ringwood Best and Fortyniner, Greene King IPA

New Forest trails around Bank

WALK

Ancient oaks, towering conifers and historic inclosures are on the route.

Woodland relics

Unenclosed woodlands such as Brinken Wood and Gritnam Wood are among the finest relics of unspoiled deciduous forest in Western Europe. Hummocky green lawns and paths meander beneath giant beech trees and beside stands of ancient holly and contorted oaks, and through peaceful, sunny glades edged with elegant silver

New Forest HAMPSHIRE

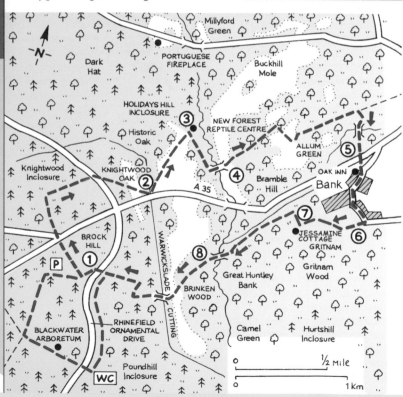

etail of a walk marker post at the New Forest 'eptile Centre

3h00	5 MILES	8 KM	LEVEL 1 2 3

SHORTER ALTERNATIVE ROUTE

1h00	2 MILES	3.2 KM	LEVEL 1 2 3

WALK

New Forest HAMPSHIRE

MAP: OS Outdoor Leisure 22 New Forest

START/FINISH: Brock Hill Forestry Commission car park; grid ref: SU 266057

PATHS: grass and gravel forest tracks, heathland paths, some roads

LANDSCAPE: Ornamental Drive, ancient forest inclosures and heathland

PUBLIC TOILETS: Blackwater car park, near start of walk

TOURIST INFORMATION: Lyndhurst, tel: 023 8028 2269

THE PUB: The Oak Inn, Bank

❶ Extreme caution needed when crossing the busy A35 (twice). Blind bends on the lane through Bank. Follow directions carefully – unsigned paths, tracks and forest rides

Getting to the start

Look for signs to the Rhinefield Ornamental Drive, off the A35 Lyndhurst-to-Christchurch road, 3 miles (4.8km) south west of Lyndhurst. Parking is signposted on the right, a short distance off the A35.

Researched and written by:
David Hancock, Peter Toms

irch. 'Inclosures' are areas of managed voodlands where young trees are protected rom deer and ponies. Areas of oak trees vere first inclosed in the late 17th century o provide the timber needed for the ;hipbuilding and construction industries. Holidays Hill Inclosure dates from 1676.

Soon after beginning the longer walk vou'll pass the most famous and probably :he oldest tree in the forest, the Knightwood Oak. It is thought to be at least 350 years old and owes its great age to pollarding (cutting back) its limbs to encourage new branches for fuel and charcoal.

Marvel at this fine tree before walking through Holiday Hills Inclosure to view the New Forest reptillary. Set up to breed rarer species for the wild, including the smooth snake and sand lizard, it offers the opportunity to view some of the forest's more elusive inhabitants.

At the end of Rhinefield Ornamental Drive is the Rhinefield House Hotel, a flamboyant Jacobean-style house, of 1890.

the walk

1 Take the gravel path at the top end of the car park (to the right of 'The Tall Trees Trail' sign), parallel with the road. In 100yds (91m) turn right and descend to a gravel track. Cross straight over then, where it curves left, keep ahead to a gate and the A35. Cross over, go through a gate and keep to the track, uphill to a junction. Turn right and follow the path to a road. Cross into Knightwood Oak car park and follow the signs to the **Knightwood Oak** itself.

2 From the oak bear right down a wide ride. Go through a gate and walk along

the path through more open woodland and bear right towards the A35. Just before a gate and the A35 take the narrow path left. Cross a **footbridge** and turn left along the line of a **drainage ditch**. Maintain this direction to a cottage and turn left to reach the **New Forest Reptile Centre**.

3 Walk back along the access drive, passing **Holiday Hills Cottage**. After 300yds (274m), at a barrier on your left, drop down on to a path and follow it across a **bridge**.

4 Keep to the main path across several clearings, and at the top of a rise fork right. In 25yds (23m) turn right, ultimately descending to and skirting left around cottages and **Allum Green**. Gently climb through trees to a defined crossing of paths and turn right. Shortly, bear half-right across a clearing and **concrete footbridge**, then continue through the woodland edge to a **telegraph pole**. Bear right for 50yds (46m), then left through a gate to the A35.

5 Turn left, then almost immediately right across the road to a gate. Walk ahead to a garden boundary and turn right, the narrow path leading to a lane in Bank. Turn right, pass the **Oak Inn** and walk through and up out of the hamlet. Just before a sharp left-hand bend (by a **cattle-grid**), bear off right beside a barrier and walk straight ahead on a wide path.

6 Go through trees and scrub to a fork on the edge of a clearing. Keep right to follow the path between an oak and a holly tree. Follow the path down past **Dell Cottage** and along the drive to a metalled lane at **Gritnam**.

7 Turn left, and after 100yds (91m), before a bridge, turn right to a **telegraph pole**. Follow the path and turn left along the gravel track to the **water treatment works**. Keep to

its left and continue into thicker woodland (mainly birch). The woods soon become mor open. Cross a **footbridge** and immediately turn left. In 25yds (23m) fork right.

8 Walk through **Brinken Wood** and acros a clearing to a bridge over **Warwickslad Cutting**. Bear right, go through a gate and turn sharp right at the gravel track. Swing left back to **Brock Hill car park**.

Short walk option

From Point 1, locate the **Tall Trees Trail pos** at the top end of the car park and follow th gravel path to the road and cross straight over. Keep to the gravel trail (marked by **red-banded posts**) as it curves right and runs parallel with the road. Pass through an impressive mixed wooded area, the pat meandering gently downhill to **Blackwater car park**. Make for the car park entrance and cross the road, signposted 'Blackwater Arboretum'. Shortly, turn right to explore th Tall Trees Trail further and return to the track, or go straight on through a gate into the arboretum. It is well worth exploring the various paths that criss-cross this small area, passing labelled trees and welcome benches. Exit by the far gate and keep to the gravel track to a **crossing of tracks**. Turn right and remain on this track to a second crossing of paths. Turn right, then on reaching the gravel path of the **Tall Trees Trail**, turn left back to the car park.

what to look for

You should see New Forest ponies grazing the lawns and trees as you cross the heath and scrub near Allum Green. They are descendants of a wild breed peculiar to the New Forest and belong to local commoners. Around 3,500 ponies graze the open forest. On the Tall Tree Trail look for the 150ft (46m) tall Douglas fir and the giant Wellingtonias, one of which is 160ft (50m) tall.

The Oak Inn

Ponies graze and pigs run free outside this 18th-century New Forest inn, formerly a cider house, tucked away in a sleepy hamlet. Despite being off the beaten track, The Oak bustles with a welcoming mix of customers, in particular walkers exploring the Forest trails, and the pub remains a true, old-fashioned community local, complete with darts and cricket teams. Inside there are bay windows, antique pine stripped old tables, bare floorboards, ancient beams, and a host of intriguing bric-a-brac – fishing rods, stuffed fish, old ski poles – adorn ceilings and walls. In winter you'll find an effective wood-burning stove to warm your toes by, and the whole pub is blissfully free of modern electronic intrusions. Idyllically set in the Heritage Area, and with a super beer garden for summer drinking, it specialises in freshly prepared food and an ever-changing range of beer, all tapped straight from the barrel.

Food

You'll find lunchtime sandwiches, ploughman's and soups alongside

about the pub

The Oak Inn
Pinkney Lane, Bank
Lyndhurst, Hampshire SO43 7FE
Tel: 023 8028 2350

DIRECTIONS: village and pub are signposted off the A35, south west of Lyndhurst

PARKING: 25

OPEN: daily, all day

FOOD: daily, all day Sunday

BREWERY/COMPANY: free house

REAL ALE: Ringwood Best, Hop Back Summer Lightning, Bass, guest beers

DOGS: welcome inside

home-cooked ham, egg and chips, cod and chips, sausage and mash and daily specials – whole sea bass and grilled lemon sole, for example.

Family facilities

Children are welcome in the eating area of the bar until 6pm. There are no special facilities for them, but they will love the beer garden and the ponies grazing outside.

Alternative refreshment stops

Pubs and cafés in Lyndhurst.

☛ Where to go from here

Take a trip up the Bolderwood Ornamental Drive and visit the deer sanctuary near Bolderwood car park. Specially constructed platforms offer an intimate view of deer roaming the forest. The best time to see them is early morning or late afternoon.

A loop between Stockbridge and Mottisfont

A gentle ride through charming Test Valley scenery.

The Sprat and Winkle Line

This ride follows a lengthy section of the Test Way, which runs along the former railway line from Andover to Romsey. Stockbridge Station has succumbed to the bulldozers, and there's little left there to betray the trail's Victorian origins. However, the stations at Horsebridge and Mottisfont have both survived. At Horsebridge the building has been faithfully restored and now makes an unusual venue for private dining and parties. A signal box stands in the landscaped grounds alongside other reminders of a bygone age, and there's even an old London & South Western Railway carriage waiting patiently at the platform. Further down the line, two former railway cottages and the old station at Mottisfont have been converted into private homes. All these buildings are easily visible from your route, but please respect the owners' privacy.

The railway line was opened in 1865 following a turf war between two powerful railway companies. It was known locally as the 'Sprat and Winkle' line, and much of the track was laid along the route of the former Redbridge canal. Like so many rural railways, traffic declined with the growth of private motoring, and the last train ran in September 1964.

the ride

1 From the car park return to The John O'Gaunt pub and turn left along the lane towards **Houghton**. Cross the river and turn left (south) on to the **Test Way**, signed to Totton. The path drops down to join the **old railway track** before re-crossing the river and skirting the **former Horsebridge Station**. You'll glimpse the beautifully restored station buildings on your left, but take care as the trail is narrow here. Pass under the old bridge at **Brook**, and continue until the Test Way swings off to the right at **Fishing Cottage**. Follow the cycle-way straight ahead as the cottage drive bears off to the left. The trail is wider, and it's an easy ride to the car park at **Stonymarsh**, where the signposted cycle route continues for 600yds (549m) beside the main road.

2 At the end of the cycle route turn right on to the lane towards **Mottisfont**. Look out for the **old station buildings** on your right, then follow the road as it winds across the River Test, and pass the entrance to **Mottisfont Abbey**. Continue into the village and bear right past the former post office, where the road joins the route of the **National Byway**. Follow the gently undulating lane north between lush hedgerows and mature oak trees, ignoring the turnings to left and right. As you reach the overhead power lines near **Pittleworth Farm**, the hedges give way to charming views across the valley to your right.

3 Pass the turning to Broughton and East Tytherley, where the National Byway swings off to the left. Now the road begins the long, steady right-hand bend into Houghton and brings you to a junction opposite **Houghton Garage**.

4 To cut the ride in half, keep straight on towards **Horsebridge** and **King's Somborne**, returning to the start in just

| 2h00 | 12.5 MILES | 20.1 KM | LEVEL 2 |

MAP: OS Explorer 131 Romsey, Andover & Test Valley

START/FINISH: Test Way car park, Horsebridge; grid ref: SU 345304

TRAILS/TRACKS: quiet country lanes and narrow off-road cycle trail

LANDSCAPE: gently rolling countryside with tranquil river crossings

PUBLIC TOILETS: Stockbridge

TOURIST INFORMATION: Romsey, tel: 01794 512987

CYCLE HIRE: Somborne Cycles, Kings Somborne, Stockbridge, tel: 01794 388327

THE PUB: The John O'Gaunt, Horsebridge

❶ Traffic on country lanes and through Stockbridge High Street (A30). Trees and undergrowth make the Test Way narrow in places. Stamina and good traffic sense required, suitable for older family groups

Getting to the start

Horsebridge lies on a lane that loops off the A3057 between Stockbridge and Romsey, west of King's Somborne. Look out for a turning signposted 'Horsebridge and Houghton', south of the village. The Test Way car park is down a gravel track, opposite The John O'Gaunt pub.

Why do this cycle ride?

The clear, flowing waters of England's premier chalk stream are the backdrop to this delightful ride. For much of the way you'll follow a converted railway trackbed, and your route passes the lovely National Trust gardens at Mottisfont Abbey. The little town of Stockbridge is a highlight of the ride. You can also make use of a short cut to tackle the route as two shorter circuits.

Researched and written by: David Foster

under 1 mile (1.6km). To complete the full ride, turn left here towards **Stockbridge**. Follow the main road as it winds through Houghton village and continue straight past the **war memorial** opposite the Boot Inn. It's worth a short diversion to visit the lovely little church of All Saints, founded in the 12th century. The road climbs gently out of Houghton past **Houghton Lodge Gardens**. From here, it's an easy ride down to the junction with the busy **A30**.

5 Stop here, and take care as you turn right over the river bridge into Stockbridge. The broad High Street offers plenty of interest, and you may prefer to make the most of its tea rooms and individual shops by wheeling your bike along the wide pavements.

6 Continue to the roundabout at the far end of the High Street and, just before the **White Hart Inn**, turn right into **Trafalgar Way**. As the road bears right, the Test Way rejoins the old railway track straight ahead. The path is narrow and overgrown in places, but it's still an easy ride south. The trail widens out at a pair of wooden gates that mark the intersection with the **Clarendon Way** (from Winchester to Salisbury). Keep straight on, crossing the River Test on a girder bridge just before the trail rises to meet the road at **Horsebridge**. Turn left here for the short ride back to the car park.

Stockbridge

HAMPSHIRE

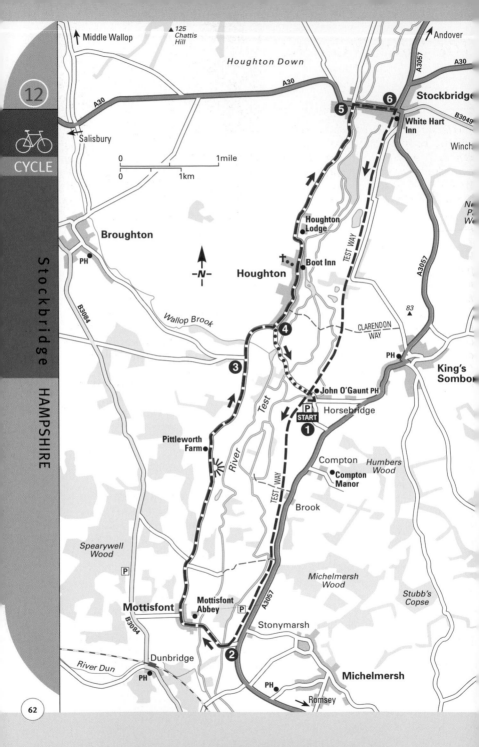

Middle Wallop

125 Chattis Hill

Andover

Houghton Down

A30

A3057

A30

A30

Stockbridge

B3049

Salisbury

White Hart Inn

Winch

0   1mile

0   1km

Broughton

PH

N—

P.
We

Houghton Lodge

B3084

Houghton

Boot Inn

TEST WAY

A3057

Wallop Brook

CLARENDON WAY

83

PH

King's Sombo

4

3

Test

River

PH

John O'Gaunt PH

P

START

1

Horsebridge

Pittleworth Farm

Compton

Humbers Wood

Compton Manor

Brook

Spearywell Wood

P

TEST WAY

Michelmersh Wood

Stubb's Copse

Mottisfont

Mottisfont Abbey

P

A3057

Stonymarsh

B3084

Dunbridge

2

River Dun

PH

Michelmersh

PH

Romsey

White cliffs, the bay and beach at Freshwater

| 4h30 | 9.5 MILES | 15.3 KM | LEVEL 1**2**3 |

SHORTER ALTERNATIVE ROUTE 1

| 3h00 | 6.5 MILES | 10.4 KM | LEVEL **1**23 |

SHORTER ALTERNATIVE ROUTE 2

| 1h30 | 3.5 MILES | 5.7 KM | LEVEL **1**23 |

MAP: OS Outdoor Leisure 29 Isle of Wight

START/FINISH: ferry terminal or pay-and-display car park opposite, Yarmouth; grid ref: SZ 354897

PATHS: disued railway, woodland and downland paths, some road walking, 4 stiles

LANDSCAPE: freshwater marsh and salt marsh, farmland, downland

PUBLIC TOILETS: at Yarmouth and Freshwater Bay

THE PUB: The Red Lion, Freshwater

⚠ Care needed crossing main roads in Yarmouth and Freshwater. Nature reserve can be wet and muddy. Long ascent up Tennyson Down on longest walk. The full 9.5-mile (15.3km) route is recommended only for more experienced older children. Only children over 10 allowed in the pub

Getting to the start

Yarmouth is 10 miles (16.1km) west of Newport on the A3054, on the north west coast of the Isle of Wight. The car park is opposite the ferry terminal. Park at the ferry terminal in Lymington and cross to Yarmouth as a foot passenger on the Wightlink ferry (www.wightlink.co.uk).

Researched and written by:
David Hancock, Peter Toms

and soon cross into the unsurfaced **Manor Road**. In 50yds (46m) bear off left, signposted **'Freshwater Way'**, and ascend across grassland towards **Afton Down**.

3 Proceed ahead at a junction of paths beside the **golf course**, and follow the gravel track right to the **clubhouse**. Go through a gate by the building and walk down the access track, keeping left to reach the **A3055**. Turn right downhill into **Freshwater Bay**.

4 For the second loop option, walk past the **Albion Hotel** and continue, turning right at Blackbridge Road, at Point 8. For the third section of the long walk, turn left instead by the **bus shelter** and public toilets, along a metalled track signposted **'Coastal Footpath'**. As it bears left, keep ahead through kissing gates and soon begin a steep ascent up a concrete path on to **Tennyson Down**. Keep to the well trodden path to reach the **memorial cross** at its summit.

5 Continue down the wide grassy swathe, which narrows between gorse bushes, to reach the replica of **Old Nodes Beacon**.

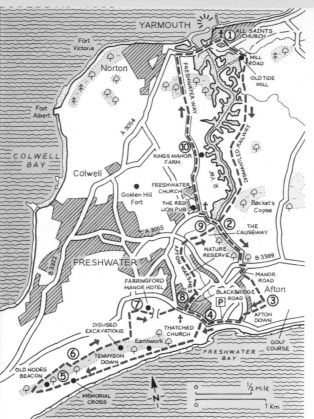

(Turn left to visit the hotel.) Turn right, pass the **thatched church**, and turn left down Blackbridge Road.

8 Just before Black Bridge, turn left into **Afton Marshes Nature Reserve**. Join the nature trail, go over the footbridge and turn left following the path beside the stream (this can be very wet) to the **A3055**. Turn left and almost immediately cross over to join **footpath F61** along the course of the old railway. After 0.5 mile (800m) reach **The Causeway**.

9 Turn left and follow the lane to All Saints Church and **The Red Lion** pub. Take the waymarked path (**Freshwater Way F1**) between a cottage and the churchyard wall. Cross two stiles and continue along the farm road. At the farmyard entrance cross the double stile on the left and bear right along the field edge to a stile.

10 At a track and the entrance to **Kings Manor Farm**, cross the stile ahead (by double gates) and follow the wide track to a gate and a junction of paths. Climb the stile on the right, pass through a copse, over another stile and bear left, uphill along the field edge. Cross a stile and maintain direction to another stile and descend into **woodland**, emerging onto a metalled track. Turn left to the **A3054** and turn right to the bridge over the River Yar, back into Yarmouth.

Here, turn very sharp right down a **chalk track**. Turn right into a car park and almost immediately ascend sharp left.

6 The path descends to a gate. Proceed along the **woodland fringe** and continue into more open countryside, then fork left at disused **excavations** on the right. Cross a stile, then keep left and after 50yds (46m) turn sharp left and descend to another stile. Cross the next field to a stile and turn right along the field edge to a stile.

7 After the next stile cross a **farm track**, go through a gate and walk along the track (F47) beside **Farringford Manor Hotel**. Pass beneath a **wooden footbridge** and continue downhill to a gate and the road.

The Red Lion

husband-and-wife team run this pub,
a picturesque setting beside All Saints
hurch. It's just a short stroll from the
dal River Yar, which makes it popular
ith the sailing set from nearby Yarmouth.
he Red Lion's origins date from the 11th
entury, though the current red-brick
uilding is much newer. The open-plan
ar is comfortably furnished with country
itchen-style tables and chairs, plus
elaxing sofas and antique pine. In addition
o the pub's four real ales, including the
sland's Goddards Best, and a good wine
election (with 16 available by the glass),
he pub is renowned for its daily
lackboard menu of interesting food.

about the pub

The Red Lion
Church Place, Freshwater
Isle of Wight PO40 9BP
Tel: 01983 754925
www.redlion-wight.co.uk

DIRECTIONS: from the A3055 east of
Freshwater by mini-roundabout and garage
follow Yarmouth signs, then turn left for the
church
PARKING: 15
OPEN: daily
FOOD: daily
BREWERY/COMPANY: Enterprise Inns
REAL ALE: Fuller's London Pride, Flowers
Original, Wadworth 6X, Goddards
DOGS: welcome in the bar

Family facilities
Children under 10 are not permitted in the
bar, but there is a fascinating dome
structure in the pretty side garden where
families can eat, also a gravelled area with
tables and chairs beyond the herb garden.

Alternative refreshment stops
Choice of pubs and cafés in Yarmouth.
Freshwater Bay has a family-friendly pub
and café, and lunch or teas can be found at
Farringford Manor Hotel.

Food
Everything is freshly made from tried and
tested recipes. Typical dishes are whole
crab salad, braised half-shoulder of lamb
with minted gravy, fresh cod and chips,
halibut with chilli and coriander sauce,
steak and kidney pie, and apple pie with
custard. Lunchtime snacks include
baguettes and ploughman's.

☛ Where to go from here
Visit the Needles Pleasure Park. Take a boat
trip to view the Needles and explore the Old
Battery, with its viewing platform and
exhibition (www.theneedles.co.uk).

A linear ride from Cowes to Newport

Take a return trip down this scenic old railway trail beside the River Medina, on the Isle of Wight.

The Ryde

Half way up the river you'll see a sad relic of former glory stuck in the mud. It's the *Ryde*, a paddle steamer built on Clydeside for the Southern Railway Company's Portsmouth-to-Ryde ferry services, and launched in 1937. Soon after the outbreak of the Second World War in 1939, the ship was requisitioned and converted for use as a Royal Navy minesweeper. Later *Ryde* was refitted with anti-aircraft weapons, and saw service defending the Normandy beaches during the D-Day invasion of Europe.

After the war *Ryde* returned to her work as an Isle of Wight ferry, but within a few years she was eclipsed by the more modern motor vessels built to replace wartime casualties. The old paddle ship found herself downgraded to summer relief duties, excursions and charters around the Solent, before she was finally withdrawn from active duty in 1968. After a couple of years moored on the River Thames as a tourist attraction, *Ryde* returned to the

Isle of Wight and was converted for use as a nightclub at the Island Harbour Marina, on the east bank of the River Medina. In 1977 she was seriously damaged by fire and, by the mid-1990s, *Ryde* lay derelict and neglected in her mud berth. Following a recent survey, there are hopes that funds might be raised to restore the old paddle steamer as a passenger-carrying vessel.

the ride

1 From Medina Road turn into Bridge Road, signposted '**Newport via cycleway**'. Follow the road all the way to the mini-roundabout at the top of the hill and turn left into **Arctic Road**, still following the signposted cycle route. Pass the **UK Sailing Academy** on your left and continue to the very end of the road.

2 Zig-zag right and left as the cycle route joins the **old railway line**, which edges its way clear of industrial Cowes through a tunnel of oak, birch and ash trees. Pass the signposted footpath to **Northwood** on your right and, a little further on, look out for the broken remains of an **old iron and timber bridge**.

3 Beyond the bridge, look out for a distinctive spire and pinnacles poking above the trees across the river. Standing little more than 0.5 mile (800m) from the gates of Osborne House, **St Mildred's church** at Whippingham was remodelled in the mid-18th century for use by the royal family. Queen Victoria gave many of the furnishings, and a permanent exhibition in the churchyard recounts the story of this extraordinary building. Continue ahead along the track.

4 Now the views begin to open up, and between Pinkmead and Stag Lane you'll spot the **old Ryde paddle steamer** slowly rusting in her mud berth at **Island Harbour Marina** on the opposite bank. This is a good area for wildlife – the hedges are thick with blackthorn, dog rose and crab apple, and in summer you'll see dragonflies and red admiral butterflies fluttering above the path. Listen, too, for the plaintive call of curlews, which use their long curved beaks to probe the mudflats for worms.

5 Now the trail crosses the **old trestle viaduct** that once carried the railway over Dodnor Creek. This area of open water, marsh and woodland was created in the 1790s when the creek was dammed to provide power for a proposed tide mill. The creek is protected as a local nature reserve and you may see reed warblers, coots, moorhens and grey herons. Beyond the creek the cycleway climbs briefly across **Dodnor Lane** and approaches the modern **industrial buildings** on the outskirts of

The harbour at Cowes

—1h45— 8 MILES — 12.9 KM — LEVEL 1 2 3 —

MAP: OS Explorer OL29 Isle of Wight
START/FINISH: Medina Road pay-and-display car park, West Cowes; grid ref: SZ 499956
TRAILS/TRACKS: back streets of Cowes, tarred and level cycle track
LANDSCAPE: wooded, riverside trail
PUBLIC TOILETS: Medina Road, Cowes, also The Quay, Newport
TOURIST INFORMATION: Cowes tel: 01983 813818
CYCLE HIRE: Funation Cycle Hire, Cowes, tel: 01983 200300 (www.funation.co.uk)
THE PUB: The Bargeman's Rest, Newport
One short hill at the start and two sections of public road. Ideal for beginners and children aged eight and over

Getting to the start

On the island, take the A3020 from Newport to West Cowes and follow signs to the floating bridge. Passengers arriving with their bikes on the Red Funnel car ferry from Southampton should follow the one-way system around to the right, and cross the floating bridge to begin the ride in Medina Road, West Cowes.

Why do this cycle ride?

This ride makes a relaxed day out, with easy access from the mainland, too. There's a lot to see from the safe, level trail, which follows the National Cycle Network route along the former Cowes-to-Newport railway line. Route finding is straightforward, and you'll enjoy some lovely views across the River Medina, with plenty of opportunities for birdwatching.

Researched and written by: David Foster

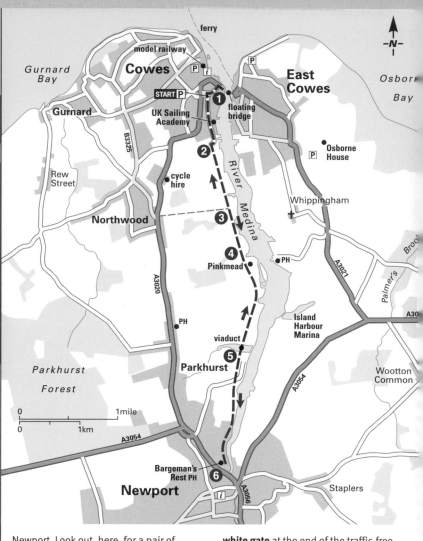

Map labels:

ferry

-N-

model railway

Gurnard
Bay

Cowes

East
Cowes

Osbor
Bay

Gurnard

START P

UK Sailing
Academy

floating
bridge

B3325

Osborne
House

Rew
Street

cycle
hire

River Medina

Whippingham

Northwood

Pinkmead

PH

A3021

Broo

Palmer's

A30

A3020

PH

Island
Harbour
Marina

viaduct

Parkhurst
Forest

Parkhurst

A3054

Wootton
Common

0   1mile
0   1km

A3054

A3054

Bargeman's
Rest PH

Newport

Staplers

A3056

Parkhurst

Newport. Look out, here, for a pair of
concrete tracks that cross the trail and lead
to a pair of slim **concrete jettie**s built out
into the river. NEG Micon is one of the
world's leading manufacturers of wind
turbines, and here a huge rolling gantry
loads their products onto waiting barges.
The facility was specially designed to
minimise disturbance to the birds that feed
on the mudflats of this internationally
protected wildlife site. Soon, reach the

white gate at the end of the traffic-free
route. Stop here, then continue straight
ahead as far as the **post-box** on the corner
of Hurstake Road. Turn left, signed to **The
Bargeman's Rest**, and bear right at the
bottom of the hill for the final 300yds
(274m) to the pub.

6 Here you can take a well-earned break
before retracing your outward route
back to Cowes.

The Bargeman's Rest

There's a distinct nautical flavour to this large pub, just a short stroll from Newport's town centre. Formerly a warehouse, the building was cleverly converted in 1999 and features pine floors, open fires and a plethora of nautical bric-a-brac, from old pictures and prints, oars and ship's wheels to lanterns, cannons and divers' helmets. The attractive paved terrace that overlooks the yachts moored beside the quay is an equally appealing spot for a relaxing pint of locally brewed Ventnor Golden. Live music is a regular feature, with jazz at lunchtime on Sundays. There are four cycle racks on the patio.

Food
The extensive menu lists the usual pub favourites, from burgers and ploughman's lunches to fish and chips, Cajun chicken and rib-eye steak – there's something for everyone here. Home-made dishes appear on the blackboard – perhaps steak and kidney pie, coq au vin or lamb rogan josh with rice and poppadoms.

Family facilities
Children are very welcome in the large family room and on the patio, which is fenced and safe for kids. You will also find a children's menu, high chairs and baby-changing facilities.

Alternative refreshment stops
Pubs and cafés in Newport.

☛ Where to go from here
Across the river, just beyond East Cowes, is Queen Victoria's seaside retreat, Osborne House, with apartments full of treasured family mementoes. The Swiss Cottage in the garden is a particular delight (www.english-heritage.org.uk).

about the pub

The Bargeman's Rest
Little London Quay, Newport
Isle of Wight PO30 5BS
Tel: 01983 525828
www.bargemansrest.com

DIRECTIONS: on the quay beside the cycleway, north east of the town centre
PARKING: 14
OPEN: daily, all day
FOOD: daily, all day
BREWERY/COMPANY: free house
REAL ALE: Ventnor Golden and Undercliff, Badger Best and Tanglefoot, guest beers

A circuit from Hamble to Bursledon

Exploring both sides of the yacht-filled Hamble estuary.

Great shipbuilders

The tidal Hamble estuary between Bursledon and Southampton Water is one of the longest in the county, and one of Britain's busiest. The river has a long history of human activity from the first Saxon settlers, who used it as a route inland, to its current status as Britain's premier yachting centre. Between the 14th and the early 19th century Bursledon and Hamble-le-Rice (its formal name) were centres for naval shipbuilding.

It was at Hamble Common in 1545 that Henry VIII watched in horror as his flagship, the 91-gun *Mary Rose*, sank just off the coast with the loss of 700 men. The Elephant Yard, next to the Jolly Sailor pub, built the 74-gun HMS *Elephant*, Admiral Nelson's flagship at the Battle of Copenhagen.

The six tiny Victory Cottages you pass in Lower Swanwick were built in the late 18th century to house shipyard workers. The bustling marinas and yacht moorings at Bursledon, best viewed from the terrace of the Jolly Sailor, have only appeared in the last 70 years. Today the villages of Hamble and Old Bursledon are a delight to explore. Hamble has a twisting main street, lined with pretty Georgian buildings, leading down to the Quay with lovely river views. Old Bursledon has a High Street but no shops, just peaceful lanes dotted with interesting buildings. Look out for the timber-framed Dolphin, a former pub. Tucked away on the slopes above the river, you'll find it a pleasure to stroll through lanes leading nowhere, especially if you pause at the Hacketts Marsh viewpoint.

the walk

1 From the quayside car park walk to the pontoon and take the **passenger ferry** across the estuary to Warsash (weather permitting, Monday–Friday 7am–5:15pm; Saturday, Sunday 8:30am–6pm). Turn left along the **raised gravel path** beside the estuary and mudflats. Cross a footbridge and continue to a gravelled parking area. During exceptionally high tides the path may flood, so walk through the car park and rejoin it by the marina.

2 At a **boatyard** keep right of a boat shed. Bear left beyond, between the shed and TS Marina, and bear right in front of the sales office to rejoin the path. On joining the road, carry straight on between industrial buildings to the **A27**.

Above: The quayside at Hamble
Right: Walking near the boats moored at Warsash on the River Hamble

3h00 — **6 MILES** — **9.7 KM** — **LEVEL 1**23

3 Turn left and cross **Bursledon Bridge**. (Turn right before the bridge to visit the historic Bursledon Brickworks.) Pass beneath the railway and turn left, signed to the station. Turn left into **Station Road**, then left again into the station car park, following signs for **The Jolly Sailor** pub. Climb a steep path to the road. Turn left at the junction, then left again to reach the pub.

4 Return along the lane and fork left along the High Street into Old Bursledon. Pause at the bench and viewpoint at **Hacketts Marsh**, then bear left at the phone-box along the High Street. Pass the Vine Inn and Salterns Lane into Kew Lane, then at a right bend, bear off left by **'The Thatched Cottage'** (that isn't!) along a footpath.

5 Join a metalled lane beside the drive to the **Coach House** then, as the lane curves left, keep ahead beside a house called **Woodlands**. Follow the path downhill to a stream. Proceed uphill through woodland (**Mallards Moor**). At a junction of paths on the woodland fringe, bear left with the bridleway, then at a concrete road turn right, then left to join a fenced path between fields.

MAP: OS Outdoor Leisure 22 New Forest

START/FINISH: pay-and-display car park by the Quay, Hamble; grid ref: SU 485067

PATHS: riverside, field and woodland paths, some stretches of road

LANDSCAPE: river estuary, farmland dotted with patches of woodland

PUBLIC TOILETS: Hamble

TOURIST INFORMATION: Hamble Valley, tel: 0906 6822001

THE PUB: The Jolly Sailor, Bursledon

🛈 Great care required along the estuary, especially at high tide, and along the roads at Hamble and Bursledon. An easy but fairly long walk

Getting to the start

The large village of Hamble is situated east of Southampton at the end of the B3397, 4 miles (6.4km) south of the M27, junction 8. At the mini-roundabout in the centre of Hamble take the narrow lane downhill to reach the Quay and car park.

Researched and written by:
David Hancock, Peter Toms

Hamble **HAMPSHIRE**

6 Cross a railway bridge and soon pass a barrier to a road. Keep left and after a sharp left-hand bend, look out for a waymarked footpath on your right and follow this path behind **houses** for 0.5 mile (800m).

7 Join a metalled path and proceed around modern housing to the end of a **cul-de-sac**. Follow this out to Hamble Lane, opposite **St Andrew's Church** and turn left to join the High Street. At the roundabout, bear right down Lower High Street back to the Quay and car park.

what to look for

Just before high tide you may see up to 12 species of wader, including dunlin, redshank, lapwing and curlew, and wildfowl – shelduck, teal and Brent geese (in winter) – feeding on the rich mudflats as you stroll the riverside path.

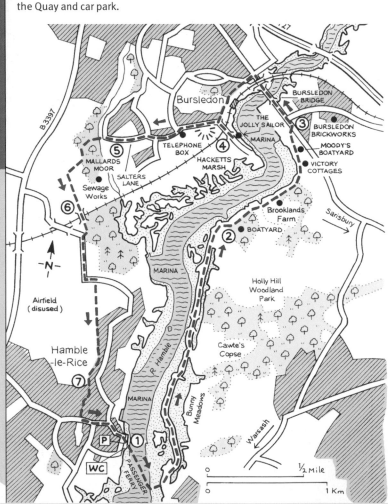

Hamble HAMPSHIRE

The Jolly Sailor

In a hard-to-top location overlooking the Hamble marina, the Jolly Sailor is a cracking pub in which to while away an afternoon. It has a splendid bench-filled front terrace and covered jetty to sup a pint on and watch the nautical world go by. Built as a shipbuilder's house in 1700, it has been a retreat for yachtsmen since Nelson's era, and was immortalised on TV as a set for Howard's Way, BBC's salty soap of the late 1980s. There's a nautical flavour to the decor in the airy front bar, with pictures of ships, nets and shells, as well as comfortable modern furnishings and sought-after bay window seats. There's a separate beamed and flagstoned back bar with a big open fire. Note the small rear garden and 100-year-old tree, and the 40 steps down and back to the pub entrance!

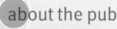

☞ **Where to go from here**
Bursledon Windmill is Hampshire's only working windmill and you can buy traditional stoneground flour made from locally grown wheat (www.hants.gov.uk/museum/windmill).

Food
Menus include ploughman's lunches and chunky bloomer sandwiches for a light bite, with sausage and mash, fish pie, moules marinière and daily specials such as chorizo confit cod, and the speciality bouillabaisse for something more substantial.

Family facilities
Families are welcome in the non-smoking area of the pub and children have a 'mini-menu' to choose from. Children need to be supervised at all times on the waterside terrace and pontoon.

Alternative refreshment stops
There's a range of pubs and tea rooms in Hamble, notably the Compass Point Café, Village Tea Rooms and the Bugle. There is also the Vine pub in Old Bursledon.

Hamble · **HAMPSHIRE**

about the pub

The Jolly Sailor
Lands End Road, Old Bursledon, Southampton Hampshire SO31 8DN
Tel: 023 8040 5557

DIRECTIONS: follow signs for the railway station off the A27 in Bursledon, 2 miles (3.2km) from the M27, junction 8	
PARKING: use railway station car park	
OPEN: daily, all day	
FOOD: daily, all day	
BREWERY/COMPANY: Hall and Woodhouse Brewery	
REAL ALE: Badger Best, Tanglefoot and Fursty Ferret, King and Barnes Sussex	
DOGS: welcome inside	

A walk around the Alresfords

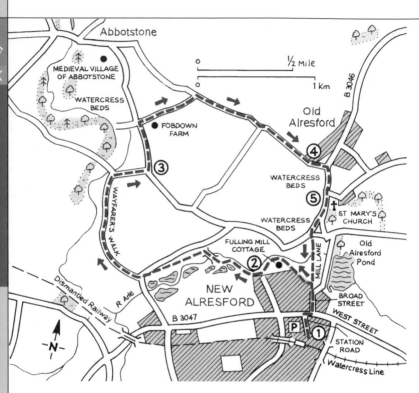

Exploring the 'new market' town at the heart of Hampshire's watercress industry.

The watercress capital

New Alresford (pronounced Allsford) is not very new at all. In fact, this delightful place, one of Hampshire's most picturesque small towns, was 'new' in 1200, when Godfrey de Lucy, Bishop of Winchester, wanted to expand the original Alresford. He dammed the River Arle, creating a 200-acre (81ha) pond, and built a causeway (the

Great Weir) to link Old Alresford with his 'New Market', as it was first called.

Most of the medieval timber-framed houses were destroyed by two devastating fires during the 17th century. As a result, much of the architecture is Georgian, notably along sumptuous Broad Street which is lined with limes and elegant colour-washed houses. New Alresford continues to be prosperous and a stroll around the three principal streets reveals the traditional country town shops plus specialist clothes, antiquarian books and craft shops.

Close to both Old and New Alresford you will find an intricate network of crystal

1h45 — 4 MILES — 6.4 KM — LEVEL 1 2 3

clear chalk streams, rivulets and channels that form the rivers Arle and Itchen and the Candover Stream. Since Victorian times these springs and rivers have played a vital role in the production of watercress. Surprisingly, watercress never stops growing in the spring water that emanates from the ground at a constant 51°F (10°C) all year. These ideal conditions made Alresford the 'Watercress Capital' of England, with the railway transporting watercress across the country. The watercress beds continue to thrive in this health-conscious age.

the walk

1 From the car park walk down Station Road to the T-junction with West Street. Turn right, then left down Broad Street and keep left at the bottom along Mill Hill. Half-way down follow the **Wayfarer's Walk marker** left down Ladywell Lane and soon

Colour-washed houses along Wayfarer's Walk in New Alresford

MAP: OS Explorer 132 Winchester
START/FINISH: pay car park off Station Road, New Alresford; grid ref:SU 588325
PATHS: riverside paths, tracks, field, woodland paths and roads
LANDSCAPE: river valley and undulating farmland dotted with woods
PUBLIC TOILETS: New Alresford
TOURIST INFORMATION: Winchester, tel: 01962 840500
THE PUB: The Globe on the Lake, Alresford
🛈 Alresford can be busy with cars; riverside paths are near water in places; take care crossing the B3046. Suitable for all ages.

Getting to the start
New Alresford is signposted off the A31 between Winchester and Alton, 6 miles (9.7km) east of Winchester. On the main village street, follow signs to the Watercress Line to locate the parking area.

Researched and written by:
David Hancock, Peter Toms

join the riverbank and pass the timbered and thatched **Fulling Mill Cottage** which straddles the River Arle.

2 Continue to the bottom of Dean Lane and turn right, keeping to the riverside path. Cross a footbridge over the river, and ascend to pass some **cottages**. Shortly, follow the footpath alongside a private drive, bear off to the left and follow it along the field edge. Join a minor road and shortly bear right up a stony track, signed **Wayfarer's Walk**. At a junction of tracks

turn right (the Wayfarer's Walk goes left) and ascend to a minor road.

3 Turn left, descend to **Fobdown Farm** and take the lane on the right beside the farm buildings, signposted '**Right of Way**'. Continue along the stony track, then on reaching a T-junction of tracks, turn right and follow the established track for just over 0.5 mile (800m), gently descending into **Old Alresford**.

4 Pass **watercress beds** on your right, and follow the now metalled lane left, past houses. Turn right beside the **green** to the B3046. Cross straight over and up to the metalled path, turning right to reach a lane opposite **St Mary's Church**.

5 Having visited the 18th-century church, cross the road and turn left along the pavement to a **grass triangle** by a junction. Bear right along the lane and take the footpath ahead over a stream and beside watercress beds back to **Mill Lane** and Broad Street.

what to look for

Explore the handsome village streets and note the Old Sun, a former pub, in East Street, where John Arlott, the cricket commentator and writer, lived for most of his life. In the churchyard you'll find the graves of French prisoners of war, who died in the village while on parole during the Napoleonic Wars. More unusually, the grave of a stray dog called Hambone Junior can be found close to the banks of the River Arle. The dog was adopted by American soldiers waiting at Alresford for the D-Day invasion in June 1944, but it was run over and killed.

Fulling Mill, Alresford

The Globe on the Lake

This 17th-century dining pub is located at the bottom of Alresford's superb Georgian main street in an enviable location beside Alresford Pond, complete with swans and dabbling ducks. The waterside garden is a splendid summer spot for an alfresco drink or meal and children will be amused by the ducks which sunbathe between the picnic benches. Inside the character bar a log fire blazes on cooler days, and the terracotta walls display a selection of interesting artworks. A smart dining room and unusual garden room share the outlook over the water. There's a good range of ales on handpump, and a blackboard above the bar lists some 20 wines by the glass.

Food

Modern seasonal menus make good use of fresh local produce, including watercress, hand-made sausages, trout, organic Hampshire lamb and game from nearby shoots. Typically, expect hake in beer batter with home-made tartare sauce, oven-roasted partridge and home-made lasagne. Lunchtime sandwiches and salads.

Family facilities

Head for the lakeside garden on sunny days where there is a playhouse for children. Children are welcome inside away from the bar. A menu and smaller portions are offered and high chairs, baby-changing facilities and small cutlery are provided.

Alternative refreshment stops

Also in Alresford are the Horse and Groom and the Bell Inn. For good light lunches there's the Broad Street Brasserie and, for coffee or tea, try Tiffins Tea Room or Tiggy's Café

☛ Where to go from here

Enjoy a nostalgic steam train ride for 10 miles (16.1km) through rolling countryside on the Watercress Line between New Alresford and Alton, which stops in between at Ropley and Four Marks (www.watercressline.co.uk).

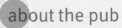

about the pub

The Globe on the Lake
The Soke, Broad Street
Alresford, Hampshire SO24 9DB
Tel: 01962 732294
www.globeonthelake.co.uk

DIRECTIONS: at the bottom of Broad Street by Alresford Pond

PARKING: use the village car park or park in Broad Street

OPEN: daily, all day Saturday and Sunday in summer, and also Sunday in winter

FOOD: as above, but no food Sunday evening in winter

BREWERY/COMPANY: free house

REAL ALE: Wadworth 6X, Courage Directors, Brakspear Bitter, Fuller's London Pride

DOGS: welcome in the garden only

Through the Meon Valley from Soberton

CYCLE

Meon Valley HAMPSHIRE

Country lanes and an old railway trail lead you through the wooded Meon Valley.

The Meon Valley Railway

On your way through Brockbridge you'll pass the former Droxford Station, where a plaque beneath the post-box records the railway's contribution to victory in the Second World War. Early in June 1944, Sir Winston Churchill and his War Cabinet met with other Allied leaders in a special train at Droxford station to plan the D-Day invasion of Europe. The Meon Valley Railway's easy curves and wide bridges reflect its promoters' aspirations for a new main line to the south coast. Yet commercial realities dictated that the railway was opened with just a single line, and this quiet rural backwater was never upgraded to double track.

As well as the five stations between Alton and Fareham, goods sidings were opened at Farringdon and Mislingford, the latter handling traffic from the local timber trade that still continues to this day. As you enter Mislingford goods yard, look out for the remains of the Southern Railway loading gauge on your right – a curious concrete structure that resembles an old-fashioned gibbet. A curved metal bar once hung from this framework, at the correct height to check that loaded wagons emerging from the sidings would pass safely under bridges and tunnels on the line.

the ride

1 Outside The White Lion, turn left on to the village's main street, heading north towards **Brockbridge**. Go over the crest of the gentle hill, then enjoy the easy 1-mile (1.6km) ride down to the former **Droxford railway station**, on your left just before the junction with the B2150.

2 Turn left here under the old railway bridge, then immediately right into **Brockbridge Road**. After a short climb you can settle down for the pleasant ride into **Meonstoke**. Continue up the gently rising village street, then fork right towards **Pound Lane** and Stocks Farm. Almost at once bear left into **Rectory Lane**, and follow it through to the T-junction opposite Stocks Meadow.

3 Turn right and climb the short hill. After 400yds (366m) bear right under the **broken railway bridge**, then right again up the slope on to the old railway line. Bear left at the top on to the broad Meon Valley

The parish church and water meadows at Meonstoke

Trail, which follows the old line south through a tunnel of trees towards Droxford. Pass under two brick arches before approaching the former **Droxford Station** on a girder bridge over the B2150.

4 Follow as the trail swings right and skirts around the **station buildings** – now converted into a private house – before rejoining the old line and continuing as before. After 400yds (364m) an elegant **brick arch** carries a footpath overhead. A further 0.75 mile (1.2km) brings you to **Cut Bridge**.

5 For a shorter ride, you can climb up to the road here and cycle back past the church to **The White Lion** at Soberton. For the full route, continue under Cut Bridge and on for a further 2 miles (3.2km) to reach the former goods yard at **Mislingford**. There are some attractive gardens behind **Bridge Cottage** on your left, just before you pass under the brick arch bridge and

2h00 **9.75 MILES** **15.7 KM** **LEVEL 1 2 3**

MAP: OS Explorer 119 Meon Valley

START/FINISH: by the White Lion, Soberton; grid ref: SU 610168

TRAILS/TRACKS: wide off-road cycle trail (may be muddy after rain) with optional return on quiet country lanes

LANDSCAPE: rolling farmland and wooded hillsides frame the little river valley

PUBLIC TOILETS: Forestry Commission picnic site, Upperford Copse

TOURIST INFORMATION: Petersfield, tel: 01730 268829

CYCLE HIRE: Owens Cycles, Petersfield, tel: 01730 260446

THE PUB: The White Lion, Soberton

🛈 Three short, steep hills, and traffic on the lanes and at the B2150 crossing in Droxford. Cycle trail may be muddy after rain. Suitable for older children with stamina and good traffic sense.

Getting to the start

The hamlet of Soberton lies south east of Droxford, on a minor road off the A32. Park considerately in the village.

Why do this cycle ride?

This varied ride loops north through the villages of Brockbridge and Meonstoke before turning south along the cycle track that follows the former Meon Valley railway line. The trail leaves the old railway at the former Mislingford goods yard, and returns to Soberton along quiet country lanes. You can easily cut the route short if you wish, and there's also an optional diversion to the woodland picnic area at Upperford Copse.

Researched and written by: David Foster

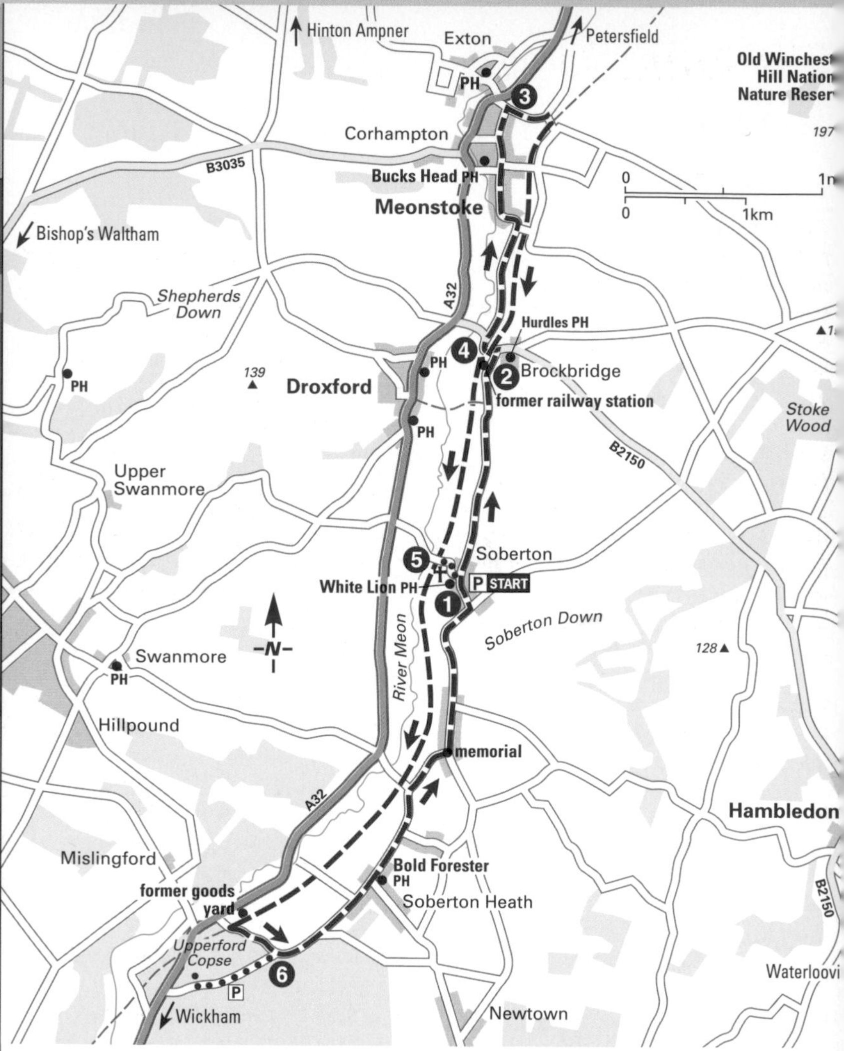

↑ Hinton Ampner   Exton   ↗ Petersfield

Old Winchest
Hill Nation
Nature Reser

197

PH

❸

Corhampton

B3035

Bucks Head PH

Meonstoke

0   1n
0   1km

↙ Bishop's Waltham

Shepherds
Down

A32

Hurdles PH

139
▲   Droxford   ❹   ❷   Brockbridge

PH   former railway station

Stoke
Wood

PH

PH

▲1

Upper
Swanmore

B2150

Soberton

❺

White Lion PH   ❶   P START

Soberton Down

128 ▲

Swanmore
PH

River Meon

↑
–N–
↓

Hillpound

memorial

A32

Hambledon

Mislingford

Bold Forester
PH

former goods
yard

Soberton Heath

B2150

Upperford
Copse

❻

Waterloovi

P

↙ Wickham

Newtown

into Upperford Copse. Turn hard left immediately under the bridge, make your way up the **rough woodland track** to the road, and continue to the junction at the top of the hill.

❻ A right turn here towards **Wickham** gives a short diversion to the Forestry Commission's **woodland picnic area** and toilets at Upperford Copse, about 0.33 mile (0.5km) down the road. To continue the

main ride, turn left towards Soberton and follow the road past the **Bold Forester** to the bottom of **Horns Hill**. Bear right and climb the other side of the little valley to the junction at **Soberton's war memorial**. Turn left towards Soberton, drift down the long hill to the crossroads at Soberton Down, then turn left into **School Hill** towards Soberton and Droxford for the final 300yds (274m) back to The White Lion.

The White Lion

The White Lion is a traditional country pub, situated near the church and opposite the village green, smack on the Wayfarer's Walk long-distance path. A 17th-century building, it has a cream-painted façade brightened by flower tubs and hanging baskets. A side patio and secluded rear garden provide peaceful summer alfresco seating. The wood-floored main bar is rustic in style, with a wood-burning stove, simple wall benches, traditional pub games and a friendly atmosphere, while the carpeted lounge and dining areas are decorated with a range of prints and warmed by an open log fire.

about the pub

The White Lion
School Hill, Soberton
Hampshire SO32 3PF
Tel: 01489 877346
www.whitelionsoberton.com

DIRECTIONS:	see Getting to the start
PARKING:	roadside parking
OPEN:	daily, all day
FOOD:	daily
BREWERY/COMPANY:	free house
REAL ALE:	Bass, Palmers 200, White Lion Bitter, guest beer

Food

Expect traditional pub meals, with the lunchtime menu listing home-cooked pies (beef, stout and Stilton), pasta meals, ploughman's lunch, a daily roast, and hot filled paninis with salad. Including locally reared water buffalo (from Broughton Manor Farm) and ostrich (from Tapnage Farm), the evening menu may offer roast salmon on fennel with dill and lemon sauce or perhaps buffalo with wild mushroom, marsala and mustard sauce.

Family facilities

Children are welcome in the eating areas.

Alternative refreshment stops

Pubs along the way include the The Hurdles at Droxford and the Bucks Head in Meonstoke.

☛ Where to go from here

To the north of here, just off the A272, Hinton Ampner is a restored Regency mansion with superb gardens which combine formal design with delightfully informal planting (www.nationaltrust.org.uk).

Meon Valley meander

Old Winchester Hill is a favoured haunt of historians and naturalists.

Old Winchester Hill

The hill dominates the Meon Valley. From its summit, some 646ft (197m) above sea level, you have magnificent views. It attracted early settlers and the remains of the fort on the summit date back to the Iron Age. Its defences comprise a massive single bank and ditch enclosing about 14 acres (4 ha), with entrances to east and west. The oval-shaped fort overlies a pattern of prehistoric fields and you will notice some large Bronze Age burial mounds, erected on the crest of the hill between 4,500 and 3,500 years ago.

Old Winchester Hill is now a National Nature Reserve, cared for by English Nature. The sheep-grazed chalk down, with its mix of open grassland, scrub and woodland, is home to rare butterflies and chalk-loving flowers. Walk here in early summer and the hill fort is dotted with fragrant orchids, while in July look out for the rare bright blue round-headed rampion.

On a warm August day the grassland is a sea of colour with hundreds of flowers, plants and wild herbs while the air shimmers with chalkhill blue butterflies. Longer grass attracts hedge and meadow browns and marbled white butterflies.

Bird-lovers should bring binoculars – you may see a peregrine falcon, buzzards soaring high, and summer migrants like the redstart and pied flycatcher. In winter fieldfares and redwings feed in numbers on the abundant berries on the stunted juniper bushes, while the yew woods provide shelter to titmice and goldcrests.

the walk

1 From the car park go through the gate onto the open down and turn left by the nature reserve's **information boards**. Follow the path around the perimeter of the reserve. Merge with a track and bear right towards the **hill fort**. Go through a gate, bear left, then right across the centre of the hill fort.

2 Fork left as you leave the ramparts and head downhill to a **stile**. Walk down a woodland path and emerge beside a gate. Continue downhill, then turn right around the edge of two fields and bear left on to a track. At a junction turn left along a **track**.

3 Where this enters a field, keep ahead along the **stony path** (parallel path if wet). Pass under the **disued railway** (or use the steps to cross the old track bed), and continue to a T-junction.

4 Bear right and cross the **footbridge** over the River Meon to the A32. Cross straight over into Church Lane and continue into **Exton**. Turn left along Shoe Lane. Go right at the junction beyond **The Shoe Inn**, and then bear left along **Allens Farm Lane**.

Left: The view from Old Winchester Hill
Below: Walking in Exton village

WALK

Meon Valley

HAMPSHIRE

(2h15)—(5.5 **MILES**)—(8.8 **KM**)—(**LEVEL** 12**3**)

MAP: OS Explorer 119 Meon Valley

START/FINISH: English Nature car park off Old Winchester Hill Lane; grid ref: SU 645214

PATHS: field paths, footpaths, tracks and sections of road, 9 stiles

LANDSCAPE: chalk downland, gently rolling farmland and river valley

PUBLIC TOILETS: none on route

TOURIST INFORMATION: Petersfield, tel: 01730 260446

THE PUB: The Shoe, Exton

❶ Great care needed when crossing the A32 (twice). Very stony and uneven path down to Exton and a long steady climb to the finish. Suitable for more experienced children

Getting to the start

Meonstoke lies between Winchester and Havant. North of Meonstoke, take a minor lane east off the A32 near the George & Falcon at Warnford, to reach Old Winchester Hill in 2 miles (3.2km). The parking area is well signed on the right.

Researched and written by:
David Hancock, Peter Toms

what to look for

Take a close look at Corhampton Church. Built on an artificial mound, it is remarkable in having no dedication, and has remained almost unaltered since it was built in the early 11th century. Many Saxon details can be seen, including characteristic 'long and short' stonework at the corners. Note too the sundial on the south wall (divided into eight sections not twelve), the 12th-century wall paintings in the chancel, the yew tree, said to be 1,000 years old, and the Romano-British coffin in the churchyard.

5 At a sharp right-hand bend keep ahead along the path beside **Exton Farm**. Go through a kissing gate and bear left along the right-hand edge of **paddocks** to a stile. Pass beside **Corhampton Farm** and church to the **A32**.

6 Cross over, walk left along the pavement and turn right by the **shop**. Take the metalled path beside the last house on your right and enter **Meonstoke churchyard**. Turn left along the lane to a T-junction beside the **Bucks Head**. Turn left, then left again at the junction. Follow the lane right (Pound Lane) and cross the **old railway**.

7 At a crossroads climb the stile on your left. Proceed ahead across the field and pass behind **gardens**, eventually reaching a stile and a lane. Climb the stile opposite and keep to the right-hand field edge to reach a stile. Maintain direction to another stile, then bear diagonally left towards a **house** and road.

8 Turn right and take the track left beside **Harvestgate Farm**. At the top of the track bear left uphill along the field edge, then first

right, following the path along the hedge into the next field. Go through the kissing gate on your left into the **Nature Reserve** an ascend steeply to the hill fort ramparts.

9 Pass through a gate and go right to joi the outward route by the **fort entrance**. Opposite the information board, follow a path just beneath the downland rim. Bear right over a **stile**, then turn left and retrace your steps to the car park.

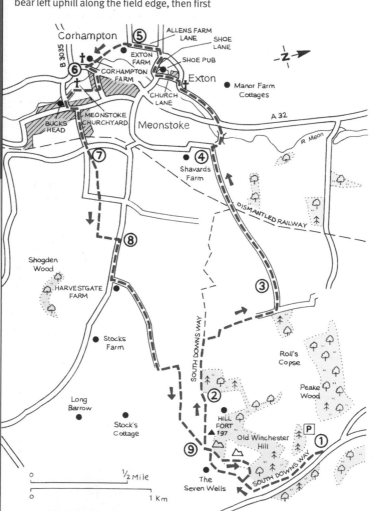

The Shoe Inn

about the pub

The Shoe Inn
Shoe Lane, Exton
Bishop's Waltham, Hampshire
SO32 3NT
Tel: 01489 877526

DIRECTIONS: Exton is just off the A32, 2 miles (3.6km) south of West Meon	
PARKING: 18	
OPEN: daily	
FOOD: daily	
BREWERY/COMPANY: Wadworth Brewery	
REAL ALE: Wadworth 6X and Henry's IPA, guest beer	
DOGS: welcome on leads in the bar and garden	

Exton's village pub used to be located in the riverside garden of today's modern-style building, but was rebuilt and relocated across the road following severe flooding in 1938. The pub's unusual name is thought to derive from being next to a former smithy. It's ablaze with colourful flowers during the summer. The interior comprises a rustic main bar and an adjacent, light oak-panelled dining area with a cosy log fire for cooler days. The real attraction in summer is the sun-trap front patio and the delightful garden across the lane beside the crystal-clear River Meon. Wiltshire brewer Wadworth owns the pub and offers its 6X and Henry's IPA on handpump, alongside a changing guest ale.

Food

Expect a good range of sandwiches, hot filled ciabattas and a choice of ploughman's, served with home-made chutney. Look to the changing chalkboard menu for salmon fishcakes with sweet pepper salsa, vegetable and herb risotto, red bream with prawns, avocado and tomato butter, or pork fillet with black pudding and a grain mustard sauce.

Family facilities

Children are very welcome in the pub and garden. There's an extensive children's menu, high chairs are available and the toilets have baby-changing facilities.

Alternative refreshment stops

The Bucks Head in Meonstoke (open all day weekends) offers an extensive menu and has a charming riverside garden.

☞ Where to go from here

Visit St John's churchyard in nearby West Meon. Here you'll find the graves of Thomas Lord, the founder of Lord's cricket ground, who retired to the village in 1830, and Guy Burgess, the former Russian agent.

Ports Down and Southwick

A rural ramble from the D-Day village of Southwick to Fort Nelson.

Ports Down and Palmerston's Follies

Ports Down rises 381ft (116m) above the coastal plain and extends for some

6.25 miles (10.1km) from Bedhampton to Fareham. It commands impressive views over Portsmouth and Langstone Harbours. This route climbs the backslope of the hill to Nelson's Monument. During the mid-19th century Britain faced the threat of a French invasion under Napoleon III. Fortifications were built around Portsmouth to protect the

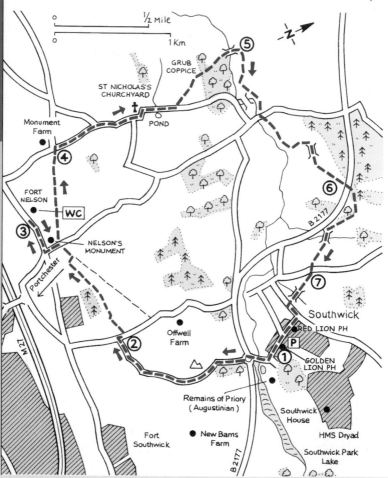

½ mile

1 Km

⑤

GRUB COPPICE

ST NICHOLAS'S CHURCHYARD

POND

Monument Farm

④

FORT NELSON

WC

③

NELSON'S MONUMENT

Porchester

B 2177

⑥

⑦

Southwick

RED LION PH

P

GOLDEN LION PH

①

Offwell Farm

②

M 27

Remains of Priory (Augustinian)

New Barns Farm

Fort Southwick

Southwick House

HMS Dryad

Southwick Park Lake

B 2177

Below: A 19th-century cannon in the grounds of Fort Nelson

naval base. Sea forts to the south of the city were bolstered by five more on Ports Down, built between 1860 and 1872. Soon after the completion of Fort Nelson in 1871 the French threat disappeared and the forts became known as Palmerston's Follies.

Hundreds of boats and thousands of men were assembled along Hampshire's low coastline and natural harbours ready for the D-Day invasion of France in June 1944. The planning of Operation Overlord was undertaken in great secrecy from the sleepy village of Southwick. On your return walk you will see a complex of modern buildings surrounding an early 19th-century mansion. The Ministry of Defence acquired Southwick House during the Second World War. Just before D-Day it became the headquarters for General Eisenhower and the Chiefs of Staff. Winston Churchill and Eisenhower supervised the landing from a special train at nearby Droxford Station.

the walk

1 From the village car park turn right to a junction and bear left to a roundabout. Go straight over taking **Crooked Walk Lane** towards Portchester. Climb steeply, bearing right by a **quarry**.

2 Where the road veers sharp left, briefly take Portchester Lane right. Almost immediately turn left through a gap in the verge and follow the footpath across a field, heading for the corner of a **copse**. Skirt the copse and cross a stile. Maintain direction towards **Nelson's Monument** across a further field to a stile and lane. Turn left, pass Nelson's Monument and turn right at the crossroads, signed to **Fort Nelson**.

| 3h00 | 6 MILES | 9.7 KM | LEVEL 1 2 3 |

MAPS: OS Explorer 119 Meon Valley
START/FINISH: free car park by the village hall, Southwick, close to HMS Dryad; grid ref: SU 627085
PATHS: field, woodland paths and stretches of road, 15 stiles
LANDSCAPE: open downland and gently rolling farmland
PUBLIC TOILETS: at Fort Nelson, only if visiting the museum
TOURIST INFORMATION: Portsmouth, tel: 023 9282 6722
THE PUB: The Red Lion, Southwick
❶ Two fairly busy sections of lane with no pavement. Suitable for older, more experienced family groups

Getting to the start
Southwick is a village north of Portsmouth. It lies just north off the B2177 between Wickham and Purbrook. In the village follow signs for HMS Dryad, to find the village hall car park.

Researched and written by:
David Halford, David Hancock

3 Having visited the fort, retrace your steps back to the **Monument** and continue down the lane for 50yds (46m). Take the footpath left over a stile. Follow the path indicated by the official diversion sign to the right corner of the **fort**, cross a stile and skirt the edge of the fort to a further stile. Bear half-right across the field, between a **house and pylon**, to a road.

4 Turn right downhill, then right again at the next junction. After 200yds (183m) bear left through **St Nicholas's churchyard**. Rejoin the road and continue past **barns** and a pond. Shortly, beside a lay-by, bear left over a stile and follow the footpath along the left-hand field edge. Continue on between fields, then by **Grub Coppice** to cross a bridge.

5 Climb a stile, and keep to the right-hand field edge to a stile on the right. Cross a further stile and walk along the left-hand field edge. Turn left across a stile by the **stream** and bear right, around the edge of the field to a stile and road. Cross the stile opposite and walk along the right-hand field edge close to a stream. Follow the **field boundary** as it swings left, pass a gate to the next field, and shortly bear right across a stile and **bridge** to join a track.

6 Pass between **farm buildings**, go through a gate and bear left down to the **B2177**. Cross over and take the footpath right along a track. It becomes grassy and bears right into **woodland**. Take the second footpath left, emerge from the trees and head across a narrow field. Cross a bridge, bear right, then half-left making for a **large oak**. Descend steps to a lane.

7 Cross over and bear half-right across the field towards the **church tower**. Cross a bridge and continue through a **plantation**. Beyond another bridge, walk up a drive to the road. Turn left, then right into **Southwick**. Keep left at the junction and left again to the car park.

The Nelson Monument rising above Fort Nelson

The Red Lion

The pretty estate village of Southwick stands on the Pilgrim's Trail from Winchester to Portsmouth, and the low-beamed Red Lion in the heart of the village is the favoured refuelling stop before the final haul up Ports Down Hill. Today, Hampshire brewer Gales owns the pub, offering tip-top pints of Butser bitter and the heady HSB to parched walkers. It is also a popular dining pub with a good, honestly priced menu. Enjoy alfresco eating and drinking on the sunny front terrace, or on the sheltered rear patio.

about the pub

The Red Lion
High Street, Southwick
Portsmouth, Hampshire
PO17 6EF
Tel: 023 9237 7223

DIRECTIONS:	see Getting to the start
PARKING:	40
OPEN:	closed Monday
FOOD:	daily
BREWERY/COMPANY:	Gales Brewery
REAL ALE:	Gales HSB and Butser, guest beer
DOGS:	allowed in garden only

Food

Firm favourites include ham, egg and chips, lambs' liver and bacon with onion gravy, and decent filling snacks such as sandwiches (smoked salmon and cream cheese), ploughman's lunches with crusty bread, salad and pickles, and filled jacket potatoes. More imaginative meals range from salmon, cod and smoked haddock fishcakes and dressed crab, to saddle of lamb stuffed with black pudding, and fillet steak with pink peppercorn sauce.

Family facilities

Although there are no specific facilities for children they are welcome inside, and smaller portions from the main menu are available.

Alternative refreshment stops

In Southwick you have the choice of two pubs – the second one is the Golden Lion. If you visit Fort Nelson, the Powder Keg Café is open all day.

☛ Where to go from here

Learn more about the events leading up to the liberation of France at Portsmouth's D-Day Museum and Overlord Embroidery (www.ddaymuseum.co.uk). The city's Historic Dockyard is home to three fabulous ships, including Nelson's flagship Victory, and the Royal Navy Museum (www.historicdockyard.co.uk).

From Hambledon to Broadhalfpenny Down

In search of the historic home of cricket.

Hambledon Cricket Club

Hambledon is steeped in cricketing history. Broadhalfpenny Down, 2 miles (3.2km) north east of the village, has echoed to the sound of leather on willow since 1750. Hambledon Cricket Club formulated the rules of the modern game and promoted the growth of club cricket. The club won 23 of 39 matches played against All England teams, and became famous throughout the world.

The Bat and Ball pub was built in 1730 and served as a pavilion and clubhouse. Landlord Richard Nyren was a great all-rounder, who became captain, secretary, groundsman and an authority on the rules of the game. When Nyren moved to the George Hotel in the village, the club continued with equal success on Windmill Down.

The gradual decline of Hambledon Cricket Club coincided with the formation Marylebone Cricket Club in 1787, and the administration of the game moving from Hambledon to Lords, the London cricket ground established by Thomas Lord, who was president of the Hambledon club at the time. When Nyren left Hambledon in 1791 the club broke up; in about 1857 a ground was established at Ridge Meadow, near Park Farm.

the walk

1 From the village hall turn left along the street into the centre and turn left opposite the **Old Post Office** towards the parish church. Follow the public footpath to the right, through the **churchyard** to Church Lane. Take the road opposite, to the right of the **infant school**, then, where it turns left, keep ahead along the well **waymarked public footpath**.

2 Cross a drive and proceed straight on between fences, with **Hambledon Vineyard** to the right. At a track turn left, then in 50yds (46m) carry straight on along the footpath. In 50yds (46m), cross a stile on your right and head towards the right-hand edge of **trees** opposite.

3 Climb a stile and bear right through the trees and over a stile into a field. Turn left along the **field edge**, and after 20yds (18m) bear diagonally right to the corner of a small fenced copse. Continue across the field, heading towards **two aerials** on the horizon, to cross a road via stiles. You are now in **Ridge Meadow**, the modern home of Hambledon Cricket Club.

WALK

Hambledon

HAMPSHIRE

4 Keep to the right-hand edge of the ground and exit in the corner, then head straight across a field and to the left of a hedge. Shortly, pass beside **woodland** then, as the path bears left, turn right through the hedge, by a **waymarker**. Proceed half-right across a large field to a stile, and straight on along a track leading to **Hermitage Farm**, following the drive out to the road.

5 Turn right for 0.5 mile (800m), then after a rise a footpath crosses the road. Turn left through the gate and bear left around the field edge to a stile. Turn right along the edge of the next field and maintain direction across three more stiles to a lane. Turn right to reach **The Bat and Ball**, the cricket ground (with its memorial stone) and crossroads.

6 Turn right, then in 250yds (229m), opposite the road to **Chidden**, cross the stile left. Head uphill across the field to a stile and turn right along a track, **waymarked Monarch's Way**. Follow the track across Broadhalfpenny Down to **Scotland Cottage**. Where the drive bears right, bear left along a tree-lined path. Gently descend for 400yds (366m) to a track and turn right.

Left: Hambledon Vineyard

2h45 — **6 MILES** — **9.7 KM** — **LEVEL 1 2 3**

MAP: OS Explorer 119 Meon Valley

START/FINISH: street parking near the village centre, Hambledon; grid ref: SU 646150

PATHS: field paths, farm tracks and stretches of road, 18 stiles

LANDSCAPE: rolling farmland and chalk down

PUBLIC TOILETS: none on route

TOURIST INFORMATION: Petersfield, tel: 01730 260446

THE PUB: The Bat and Ball, Clanfield

🛈 Care needed on the short stretches of road

Getting to the start
Hambledon is located due north of Portsmouth and south west of Petersfield, just off the B2150. Park along the main street.

Researched and written by: David Hancock, Peter Toms

what to look for
Take a closer look at Hambledon's parish church. Built around a little Saxon church, which still forms part of the nave, it is one of the most architecturally interesting in Hampshire. The various stages of development are well described in the church guidebook.

Below: Cricket at Hambledon

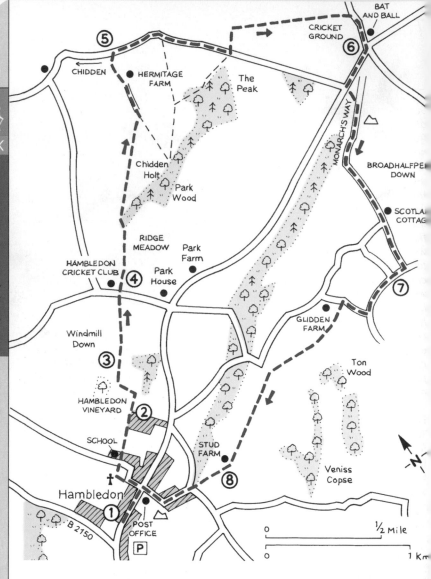

BAT
AND BALL

CRICKET
GROUND

⑤

CHIDDEN

HERMITAGE
FARM

The
Peak

⑥

MONARCH'S WAY

BROADHALFPE
DOWN

Chidden
Holt

Park
Wood

SCOTLA
COTTAG

RIDGE
MEADOW

Park
Farm

⑦

HAMBLEDON
CRICKET CLUB ④

Park
House

Windmill
Down

③

GLIDDEN
FARM

Ton
Wood

HAMBLEDON
VINEYARD

②

SCHOOL

STUD
FARM

Veniss
Copse

⑧

†

Hambledon

①

N

B 2150

POST
OFFICE

P

0   ½ Mile

0   1 Km

7 In 75yds (69m) fork left, then at a T-junction turn right to **Glidden Farm**. After a slurry pit turn left and walk down a track. Cross a stile, bear right past a **barn** and cross two more stiles. Follow the line of **power cables** across three fields and through a paddock. Walk along a track and turn right over a stile to the rear of **outbuildings** (Stud Farm) on to the access road.

8 Bear off right down a footpath to a road. Turn right and keep left **steeply downhill** back into Hambledon. Turn left through the village back to the village hall.

The Bat and Ball

about the pub

The Bat and Ball
Hyden Farm Lane, Clanfield
Waterlooville, Hampshire PO8 0UB
Tel: 023 9263 2692

DIRECTIONS: from the B2150 go through
Hambledon village, following signs to
Clanfield
PARKING: 30
OPEN: daily, and all day Saturday and
Sunday in summer
FOOD: daily
BREWERY/COMPANY: Gales Brewery
REAL ALE: Gales Butser, GB and HSB
DOGS: welcome in the bar

Standing opposite the seminal cricket pitch where the game of cricket changed from being just a pastime to being a national sport, The Bat & Ball was built in 1730 when it also served as a pavilion and clubhouse in the heyday of Hambledon Cricket Club. What better way to enjoy a relaxing pint than to watch leather hitting willow from the sunny front terrace of the pub on a summer weekend or balmy evening. If you have to sit inside, look for the collection of cricketing memorabilia adorning the walls of the bar, which includes an inscribed bat presented to Richard Nyren, landlord and greatest all-round cricketer of his day, in 1791. You'll also find three rambling bars with comfortable modern furnishings, a panelled restaurant, winter log fires, and local Gales beer on handpump.

Food
The extensive menu offers traditional pub food, and daily changing blackboards list fresh fish and seafood as a speciality. Expect good baguettes and toasted sandwiches, starters such as seafood

chowder and bruschetta, with main dishes including the likes of fisherman's pie, beef stroganoff and rib-eye steak with pepper sauce. Separate restaurant menu, and Sunday roast lunches.

Family facilities
Families are very welcome in the bars and restaurant and there's a children's menu. Plenty of seating on the front terrace and on the sheltered rear patio, with downland views.

Alternative refreshment stops
In Hambledon, try the Vine Inn (by the village hall) for home-cooked food.

☛ Where to go from here
Between Havant and Horndean, off the B2149, lies Staunton Country Park, with lakes and parkland, Victorian tropical houses and an Ornamental Farm with llamas, shire horses and pygmy goats (tel: 023 9249 8156).

Queen Elizabeth Country Park

WALK

Follow woodland and downland trails to a unique archaeological farmstead.

Queen Elizabeth Country Park

The park lies at the western end of the South Downs and forms part of the East Hampshire Area of Outstanding Natural Beauty. It covers about 1,400 acres (567ha) and is dominated by three hills: the chalk downland of Butser Hill, which at 810ft (270m) is Hampshire's second highest point, and the beautiful woodland of Holt Down and War Down.

Along with its informative Visitor Centre and café, it is the starting point for longer circular walks and more adventurous hikes along some of Hampshire's long-distance trails, including the South Downs Way, the Hangers Way and the Staunton Way.

The emphasis of this walk is on exploring the Ancient Archaeological Farm south of the park, and two of Hampshire's oldest and scenically impressive villages, Chalton and Buriton. Walk up Butser Hill for magnificent all-round views. Here you will also see signs of Bronze Age burial mounds and cross-dykes and, in spring and early summer, a wide variety of chalk-loving plants clothe the grassy slopes.

Beautiful Buriton nestles beneath the beech-clad South Downs. It features a green with a duck pond, surrounded by attractive cottages, a large church, a rectory and a stone manor house.

Along the road is St Michael's Church in Chalton, which has a fine 15th-century font – and from the top corner of the churchyard, a memorable downland view.

The reconstructed Iron Age farm below Butser Hill

the walk

1 From the car park follow the **Woodland Trail** (green-striped posts) to the right.

2 On reaching the road, turn left then right onto the gravel path. Ascend and fork right by a **'no cycling'** sign, following the track around the edge of the woods. As the track swings left around the corner of the woods, turn sharp right over a stile. Leave the Country Park and turn left onto a **bridleway**. The path undulates but soon levels and then gradually descends to a road. Note the 18th-century **windmill** on the skyline to your right.

3 At the road, turn right to visit **Butser Ancient Farm** (the footpath in 50yds/ 46m avoids the road), otherwise turn left and follow the road (some blind bends) for 0.5 mile (800m) into **Chalton**. Turn left at the junction, signed to **Ditcham**.

4 In 250yds (229m) fork left along a **byway**. Continue between fields and

what to look for

Make a point of visiting the Norman Church of St Mary in Buriton. The 18th-century historian Edward Gibbon, best known for his book The Decline and Fall of the Roman Empire, lived in the adjacent manor house and is buried in the church. You will also find a memorial window to John Goodyer (1592–1664), one of the first great botanists, who wrote about potatoes and tobacco after they were brought back to this country. Note the original paving stones from London Bridge around the font.

3h00 — **6.75 MILES** — **10.9 KM** — **LEVEL 1 2 3**

MAP: OS Explorer 120 Chichester
START/FINISH: pay-and-display car park, Queen Elizabeth Country Park; grid ref: SU 718185
PATHS: woodland paths, bridleways and forest tracks, 4 stiles
LANDSCAPE: downland forest and farmland
PUBLIC TOILETS: by visitor centre
TOURIST INFORMATION: Petersfield, tel: 01730 260446
THE PUB: The Five Bells, Buriton
🛈 Special care needed when crossing the railway line, and the lane to Chalton can be busy. Two long steady climbs and a steep ascent and descent into Buriton. Suitable for fitter, older family groups

Getting to the start
The Queen Elizabeth Country Park is between Petersfield and Horndean, signposted east off the A3, 3 miles (4.8km) south of Petersfield. The car park is beside the Country Park's visitor centre.

Researched and written by: David Hancock, Peter Toms

The view from Butser Hill in Queen Elizabeth Country Park

oon descend between trees to join a road. urn left, walking parallel to the **railway** for .25 mile (400m), to cross a stile on the ght. Bear half-left across a large field nd enter **woodland**.

5 At a junction of paths continue straight ahead and steadily climb a wide forest rack. On the descent fork left, then almost mmediately fork right down a narrow ignposted footpath to a road.

6 Turn right then, in 100yds (91m), take the **footpath** left and head steeply own through the trees to a stile. Bear half ight across a field to a stile by a gate then ollow the path round to the left, passing **pond**, into Buriton.

7 Turn left along the **High Street**. Just beyond house No. 29, take the footpath eft (or go straight on for The Five Bells ub). Go round the **village hall** and ascend longside **playing fields** to a gate. Very arefully cross the railway line, go through gate and follow the path to a junction with **bridleway**. Turn right and steeply ascend :o the road. Cross straight over into **Hall's Hill car park**.

8 Go through a gate and up a wide track (South Downs Way) back into Queen Elizabeth Country Park. Gradually ascend.

Just after a track merges from the right, fork right and descend. Go through a gate, pass through **Benhams Bushes car park**, walk down a short stretch of metalled road, then bear off left following the South Downs Way. Rejoin the road at **Gravel Hill car par** and retrace your outward route back to th car park.

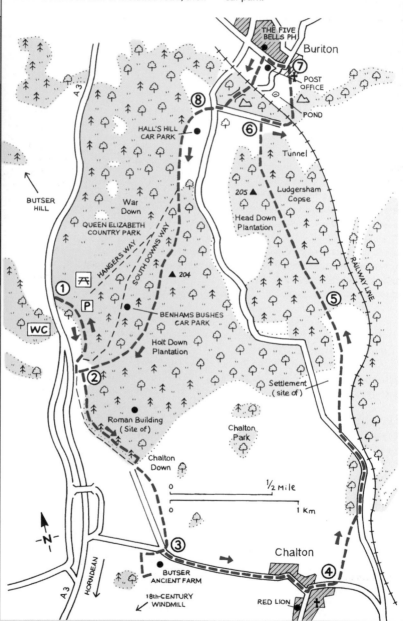

The Five Bells

The South Downs Way passes close to Buriton on its way to Winchester, and this characterful brick-and-stone inn makes a welcome refreshment stop. Dating to the 16th century, the pub offers a rustic ambience within the series of rambling, low-beamed bars. It is warmed by four large open fires and furnished with mainly sturdy pine on rug-strewn wood-block floors, making this a comfortable place. The restaurant was formerly a farrier's, then a clay pipe factory, and at one point even the village morgue! Expect the full complement of Badger ales on tap, eight wines by the glass, imaginative meals, and a sheltered summer garden with vine-bearing trellis and fruit trees.

about the pub

The Five Bells
High Street, Buriton
Petersfield, Hampshire GU31 5RX
Tel: 01730 263584

DIRECTIONS: Buriton is signposted off the A3 1 mile (1.6km) south of Petersfield or off the B2146 South Harting road south east of Petersfield	
PARKING: 12	
OPEN: daily	
FOOD: daily	
BREWERY/COMPANY: Hall and Woodhouse Brewery	
REAL ALE: Badger Best & Tanglefoot, Fursty Ferret	
DOGS: allowed in the bar and garden	

Food
A wide-ranging menu has something for all tastes, from lunchtime sandwiches and ploughman's to gardener's pie, steak and kidney pie, local game, red bream with onions and deep-fried prosciutto, and grilled whole plaice.

Family facilities
Children are welcome in the eating area of the bar. A children's menu and smaller portions are available.

Alternative refreshment stops
There is the café in the Country Park and The Red Lion at Chalton (see p103) with Gales ales and good views from the garden.

☞ Where to go from here
Uppark House, east of here at South Harting, is a 17th-century mansion owned by the National Trust, and restored with great care after a major fire in 1989 (www.nationaltrust.org.uk).

A circuit of Queen Elizabeth Country Park

A wooded ride through the heart of Hampshire's largest country park.

Butser Ancient Farm

Butser Ancient Farm was founded by Dr Peter Reynolds in 1972 to improve the understanding of prehistoric farming methods. The original farm was established west of the A3 at Rakefield Hanger, some 3 miles (4.8km) north of the present site. Although research continued at this remote location until 1989, Rakefield Hanger wasn't the ideal place to develop the farm's educational role. So, in 1976, a new site was developed at Hillhampton Down, just

across the A3 from the country park visitor centre. This site boasted a large, thatched roundhouse, with fields of crops and an industrial research area for producing charcoal and early metals like iron, copper, tin and bronze. In 1991 the farm moved to its present site at Bascomb Copse, where the buildings, animals and crops recreate the living conditions on a British Iron Age farm about 2,300 years ago. The farm has a reception area with a video introduction, souvenir shop and toilets. There's also an activity centre where visitors can try their hand at grinding corn, spinning, weaving or making clay pots. The ancient farm is open to the public between March and September for weekend events, including

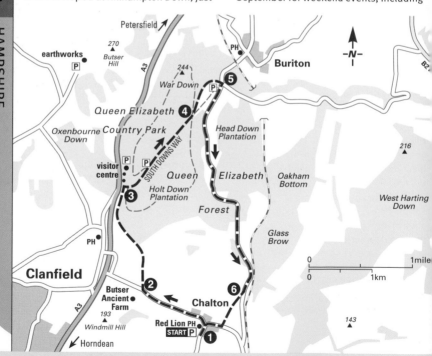

MAP: OS Explorer 120 Chichester

START/FINISH: public car park next to the Red Lion, Chalton; grid ref: SU 731160

TRAILS/TRACKS: rough off-road trails, quiet rural lanes

LANDSCAPE: thickly wooded rolling chalk hills, with open fields grazed by sheep

PUBLIC TOILETS: Queen Elizabeth Country Park visitor centre

TOURIST INFORMATION: Petersfield, tel: 01730 268829

CYCLE HIRE: Owens Cycles, Petersfield, tel: 01730 260446

THE PUB: The Red Lion, Chalton

🛈 There are two short, steep sections in the Country Park where you may prefer to push your bike; bumpy off-road tracks. Suitable for older children, some off-road experience useful

Getting to the start

Chalton lies east of the A3 between Petersfield and Horndean. Leave the A3 at the Clanfield exit, and follow signs to Chalton and the Red Lion pub (about 1 mile/1.6km). Bear right in the village and you'll find the public car park tucked away on the right hand side, just past the Red Lion.

Why do this cycle ride?

This route links Hampshire's oldest pub with its largest country park. Twenty miles of trails thread their way through the park's 1,400 acres (567ha) and you're sure to meet plenty of like-minded people enjoying themselves in the great outdoors. There's an excellent visitor centre, too, complete with shop, information desk and café. The route takes in a section of the South Downs Way national trail before returning to Chalton on a quiet country lane.

Researched and written by: David Foster

demonstrations of prehistoric cookery, textiles and clothing.

the ride

1 Leave the car park and turn left past **The Red Lion,** then left again at the junction towards **Clanfield and Petersfield.** Pass under the power lines and continue for 700yds (640m) to the bottom of the hill opposite **Butser Ancient Farm.**

2 Fork right here on to the bridleway and **off-road cycle trail,** a bumpy track with lovely views across the fields to **Windmill Hill** and the ancient farm behind you on your left. The bridleway climbs steeply as it approaches the woods at the corner of the country park, and it's probably safer to dismount and push your bike at this point. Follow the bridleway as it skirts the western edge of the forest and drops gently down to the tarred **Forest Drive** and **picnic areas.**

3 Here you can turn left for the 300yds (274m) diversion to the park's **visitor centre,** with café and toilets. Alternatively, turn right to continue your ride. This

Cycling through Queen Elizabeth Country Park

section, which follows part of the **South Downs Way** national trail, takes you past the **Benhams Bushes barbecue site** (advance booking required). Follow the Forest Drive for 600yds (549m). When you reach the hairpin bend, fork right through **Benhams Bushes car park** on to the waymarked off-road cycle trail. Follow the bumpy gravel road for just over 0.5 mile (800m) to a junction near the top of the hill.

4 Bear left here, then fork right a few yards further on, sticking with the gravel road as it drops to a **wooden gate** at the Forestry Commission's **Hall's Hill car park**. Continue through the car park and stop at the road exit.

5 Leave the South Downs Way here, and turn right on to the **narrow lane** that drops down towards Chalton and Finchdean. This easy ride takes you through a deeply rural, **wooded landscape**; sheep graze in small open fields between the beechwoods and hazel coppices, and you may spot the occasional deer. Eventually you'll pass under a line of **electricity wires**, before the road climbs around a right-hand bend and runs beside the railway for a short distance. Two hundred yards (183m) further on, look out for a **signposted byway** on your right-hand side.

6 Fork right here for the short, sharp climb up on to **Chalton Peak**. There are fine views on your right towards Windmill Hill, with dog rose, bramble and knapweed colouring the hedges beside this pleasant, level section. At the end of the byway turn right for the final 200 yds (183m) back to the junction where you fork left to return to The Red Lion and the car park.

Negotiating a bend on a woodland path in the Queen Elizabth Country Park

The Red Lion

mash with rich gravy, and puddings such as cherry pie and bread pudding.

Family facilities

Children are welcome in the dining room (where there's a small standard children's menu) and the spacious rear garden. The latter offers lovely views to Windmill Hill and Butser Ancient Farm.

This beautiful timbered and thatched pub – a typical Hampshire cottage, reputedly built in the 12th century as dwellings for the craftsmen building the parish church – stands at the heart of the quaint village, opposite the lych-gate. Tourists, walkers and weary A3 travellers are attracted into its cosy and rustic main bar and modern dining bar extension – not least for the tip-top ale and the impressive range of whiskies and country wines. Both the old-fashioned public bar and the lounge bar are contained in the original building, the high-backed old settles of the former providing the perfect foil to the black beams and huge inglenook. This is reputedly Hampshire's oldest pub, and it is immaculately maintained by the very local Gales Brewery.

Food

In addition to sandwiches and filled baguettes (hot roasted vegetables), ploughman's lunches and filled jacket potatoes, daily specials may include braised mixed game with mushrooms and red wine, local pork and watercress sausages on chive

Alternative refreshment stops

The Coach House Café in Queen Elizabeth Country Park or the Five Bells in Buriton.

☛ Where to go from here

Gale's Brewery at Horndean has tours and a shop (www.galesales.co.uk).

about the pub

The Red Lion

Chalton, Waterlooville
Hampshire PO8 0BG
023 9259 2246
www.gales.co.uk

DIRECTIONS:	in the centre of the village
PARKING:	use adjacent village car park
OPEN:	daily
FOOD:	daily
BREWERY/COMPANY:	Gales Brewery
REAL ALE:	Gales Best, Butser and HSB, guest beer

A South Downs circuit from Stoughton

Discover a magical ancient forest.

An ancient yew forest

You might not expect to find the largest yew forest in Europe at the western extremity of the South Downs, but that's exactly where it is. This remote downland landscape, covering more than 200 acres (81ha), is cloaked with 30,000 yew trees. Once a wartime artillery range, Kingley Vale became one of Britain's first nature reserves in 1952. Today, it is managed by English Nature.

Silent, isolated and inaccessible by car, the grove is a haven for ramblers and naturalists. Our walk skirts the forest, but if you have the time to explore this enchanting place, study the map closely and make up your own route.

The yew is one of our finest trees and can live up to 2,000 years. It is usually a large but squat tree, its branches and dark green needles create a dense evergreen canopy which allows little light to filter to the forest floor. With their deep red trunks, branches and shallow roots twisted into monstrous shapes, some of the yews at Kingley Vale are thought to be at least 500 years old. Even on the sunniest summer's day, the scene is eerily dark, strange and mystical, like something from the pages of a fairy story. The yew has always featured strongly in folklore, and according to legend this place was a meeting point for witches who engaged in pagan rites and wove magical spells here.

Various theories about the origin of the forest have been put forward. Some sources suggest the trees were planted to guide pilgrims travelling across the South Downs to Canterbury. Earlier, Bronze Age kings were buried here, confirmed by various tumuli on the map.

The grove teems with wildlife, and green woodpeckers are just one of 57 species of bird that breed here. The bee orchid blooms in June, and sheep and wild fallow deer keep the turf short for 200 further species of wild flower.

the walk

1 From the car park take the gravel track left (signposted '**bridleway**') and follow it away from the road, skirting dense **beech woodland**. There are striking views on the left over pastoral, well-wooded countryside. Keep right at a fork and follow the track as it curves to the right. Proceed straight on at a major junction of tracks and begin a gradual ascent beneath the boughs of beech trees.

2h00 · **4.5 MILES** · **7.2 KM** · **LEVEL 2**

2 Eventually you break cover from the trees at a major junction of waymarked tracks. Go straight on, looking to the right for spectacular views. Continue to the next bridleway sign, and fork left, joining a **path** running roughly parallel to the track. Cut between trees and keep going until, at a gap by a **marker post**, you descend the path on the right. Rejoin the enclosed track, turning left to follow it up the slope towards **The Devil's Humps**.

3 On reaching these tumuli take time to wander off the track and enjoy the magnificent vistas across the Downs. The view to the north, over remote **woodland** and downland, is impressive enough, but the panorama to the south is particularly outstanding. Immediately below you are the trees of **Kingley Vale**. Rejoin and continue along the track, passing the **nature reserve** on your left. Continue between lines of beech trees and more mixed woodland.

Left: View from Bow Hill towards Stoughton
Below: Yew trees on a trail in Kingley Vale

MAP: OS Explorer 120 Chichester, South Harting & Selsey

START/FINISH: free car park at Stoughton Down; grid ref: SZ 814126

PATHS: mostly woodland paths and downland tracks

LANDSCAPE: dense woodland and rolling downs

PUBLIC TOILETS: none on route

TOURIST INFORMATION: Chichester, tel: 01243 775888

THE PUB: Hare & Hounds, Stoughton

🛑 Care needed on the country lane out of Stoughton. Ascents and descents gentle but long

Getting to the start

Stoughton is situated between Petersfield and Chichester, signed 2 miles (3.2km) east off the B2146. Pass through Walderton and Stoughton village, and the car park at Stoughton Down is 1 mile (1.6km) further on.

Researched and written by:
Nick Channer, Peter Toms

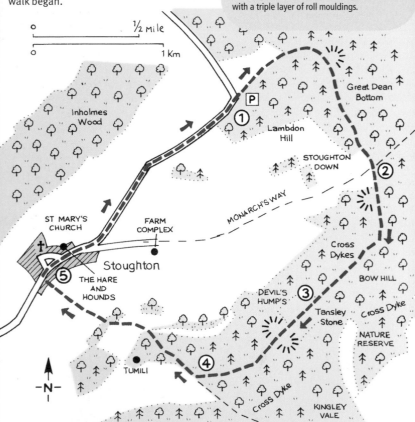

4 Turn right at the next main junction and follow the **bridle track**. On the left are glimpses of **Chichester harbour**, with its complex network of watery channels and sprawling mudflats, distantly visible on a clear day. Descend through an area of beech woods past a **memorial stone**, and keep going until you reach the road. Turn right and walk through the village of **Stoughton**.

5 Pass the entrance to **St Mary's Church** on the left, followed by the **Hare & Hounds** pub. Continue through the village and out of Stoughton. At a left-hand bend look for the entrance to the car park on **Stoughton Down** on the right, where the walk began.

what to look for

Bronze-Age barrows, known as the Devil's Humps, can be seen on Bow Hill. There are several legends on the South Downs concerning the Devil. This one suggests that anyone who runs round the humps six times will experience a sighting!

As you approach Stoughton village, look for a memorial stone on the right of the path. It was in this field, in November 1940, that a Polish pilot officer based at nearby RAF Tangmere died when his Hurricane crashed following aerial combat with a German ME109.

Take a closer look at Stoughton's 11th-century Church of St Mary. The exterior is barn-like, bulky even, and inside it is unexpectedly spacious. The south transept was converted into a tower in the 14th century, the nave is over 30ft (9m) high and there is a striking Norman arch with a triple layer of roll mouldings.

Hare & Hounds

about the pub

Hare & Hounds
Stoughton, Chichester
West Sussex PO18 9JQ
Tel: 023 9263 1433

DIRECTIONS: in the centre of the village, east of the church	
PARKING: 6	
OPEN: daily	
FOOD: daily	
BREWERY/COMPANY: free house	
REAL ALE: Fuller's London Pride, Timothy Taylor Landlord, Young's Bitter, Hampshire Rose	
DOGS: well behaved dogs welcome inside	

Food
Choose from a good snack menu, which includes sandwiches and baguettes, or go for something more substantial such as roast beef salad, lasagne or steak and mushroom pie. Everything is cooked on the premises and there are various game dishes in season, perhaps venison steak or saddle of hare. Summer specials may include fresh dressed crab and whole sea bass.

Family facilities
Although there are no special facilities for children, they are welcome inside the pub.

☞ Where to go from here
Historic West Dean Gardens lie to the east of Singleton on the A286, covering 35 acres (14ha), with a pergola by Harold Peto, mixed borders and a superb walled kitchen garden (www.westdean.org.uk).

Stoughton Is set In an extremely qulet and very beautiful spot on the lower slopes of the South Downs, and the Hare & Hounds, a striking, creeper-covered building of brick and flint, dates back to the 17th century, when it was two cottages. A pub for some 100 years, it is today a comfortably rustic village local, with each of its three interconnecting beamed rooms sporting old pews, pine tables and chairs and warming winter log fires. In summer the sun-trap front terrace is the favoured spot for weary South Downs walkers to relax and refuel. There's an equally pleasant rear garden with rural views.

The Centurion Way from Chichester

Centurion Way

WEST SUSSEX

Encounter the sculptures along the Centurion Way cycle route, and scale the Iron Age banks of The Trundle.

The Centurion Way and The Trundle

This traffic-free bike and pedestrian trail opened in full in 2002, and was named the Centurion Way because it crosses a Roman road at one point. For most of its length it follows the trackbed of a defunct railway that ran between Chichester and Midhurst. This existed from 1881 until 1957; the stretch southwards from Lavant was kept in operation for transporting sugar beet and gravel up to 1991. Along the route you will see some highly quirky modern sculptures: two of these, Roman Archway and Primary Hangers, were made with the help of local schoolchildren.

Huge grassy banks on The Trundle mark the extent of an Iron Age hillfort, which has two modern masts on it. The view is quite spectacular, including almost the entire east coast of the Isle of Wight, the watery expanses of Chichester Harbour and the stands of Goodwood racecourse. If you look carefully on a clear day, you can see the chalk cliffs of the Seven Sisters way over to the east, and the white tent-like structure of

Butlin's in Bognor Regis. There is no access for cyclists to the top, so lock up your bike by the car park and walk up.

the ride

1 Take the **Centurion Way** (signposted as cycle path to Lavant) to the right of the house at the end of the road, and to the left of the **school gates**. This joins the old railway track by a sculpture called **Roman Archway**, which spans the track. After going under a bridge, you will see the entrance to **Brandy Hole Copse**, a local nature reserve to the left. Among the oak coppice and chestnut trees are high, overgrown banks that were erected 2,000 years ago by a late Iron Age tribe as boundaries or fortifications, some years before the Roman Conquest in AD 43. Dragonflies and bats are attracted to this reserve, which also has three ponds to explore.

2 Before going under the next bridge (signposted Lavant), you will see sculptures called **The Chichester Road Gang**, resembling road workers carrying tools, but made out of metal canisters. Away to the left is another artwork called the **Roman Amphitheatre**. It is here that the now invisible Roman road once passed.

3 After the next bridge, with its **dangling metal sculptures** – Primary Hangers – the route leaves the old railway track and joins a residential road in Mid Lavant. Just down to the right is an excellent **adventure playground**. Carry along the road, following

Roman Amphitheatre is one of several unusual works of art on the route

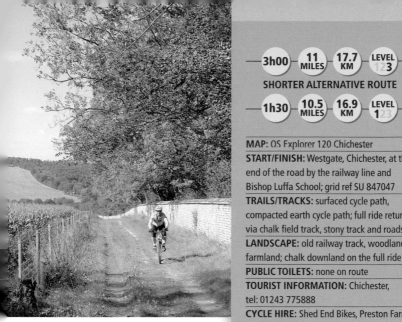

Cycling along a quiet lane on the route

| 3h00 | **11** MILES | **17.7** KM | LEVEL 12**3** |

SHORTER ALTERNATIVE ROUTE

| 1h30 | **10.5** MILES | **16.9** KM | LEVEL **1**23 |

24

CYCLE

Centurion Way

WEST SUSSEX

MAP: OS Explorer 120 Chichester

START/FINISH: Westgate, Chichester, at the end of the road by the railway line and Bishop Luffa School; grid ref SU 847047

TRAILS/TRACKS: surfaced cycle path, compacted earth cycle path; full ride returns via chalk field track, stony track and roads

LANDSCAPE: old railway track, woodland, farmland; chalk downland on the full ride

PUBLIC TOILETS: none on route

TOURIST INFORMATION: Chichester, tel: 01243 775888

CYCLE HIRE: Shed End Bikes, Preston Farm, near West Dean (on this route) tel: 01243 811766, 07946 341685

THE PUB: The Selsey Arms, West Dean

🚲 The full ride has long, stony descent: ride with care and wheel your bike if necessary. There's a short section along the main road.

Getting to the start

Turn off the A27 on the western side of Chichester, along the A259 into Chichester. Turn left at the roundabout, then left at the next mini-roundabout, along Westgate. Roadside parking at the end of the roadl.

Why do this cycle ride?

There is some weird and wonderful sculpture as well as an adventure playground along the Centurion Way, a level path shared with walkers. From the fringes of Chichester, head out into the country, reaching West Dean. Either return the same way, or take a more demanding off-road route up to The Trundle.

Researched and written by: Tim Locke

signs for West Dean. After concrete bollards, and soon after a **postbox** on the left, then St Mary's Close on the right, turn right at a **square green** to rejoin the old railway track (not signposted at time of writing). Later the Centurion Way turns left to leave the old railway track, then turns right along a cycle path parallel to the **A286**.

4 This path ends at the village of **West Dean**. Turn right along the small road, round the back of the village (take the next turning on the left for **The Selsey Arms**, or to see the churchyard, with its fine old tombstones, carry straight on). For the short route, return the same way to the start. For the full route bear to the right where the road first bends left, towards ornate **iron gates** in a flint wall. Follow the bridleway uphill, alongside the wall and along the field edge, and later through a forest. Finally emerge at the top as the view opens out by a **house**. Keep forward on a track to a car park.

5 Before turning right (towards the sea) to continue, walk up ahead to the summit of **The Trundle**, marked by two prominent **masts**, to enjoy the view. Now carefully ride the stony route down a long hill to **East Lavant**. Turn right along the main village street, avoiding a left fork, and past the Royal Oak. Ignore side turns and go past a **triangular recreation ground** on your right.

6 Turn left along the **A286** for 350 yards (320m). Take the first turning on the right (with the cycle route sign for Chichester) by stopping at a small lay-by (just before this turning) on the left and then crossing the road when it is safe to do so. After crossing the bridge, turn left to rejoin the **Centurion Way**, and turn right to return to the start.

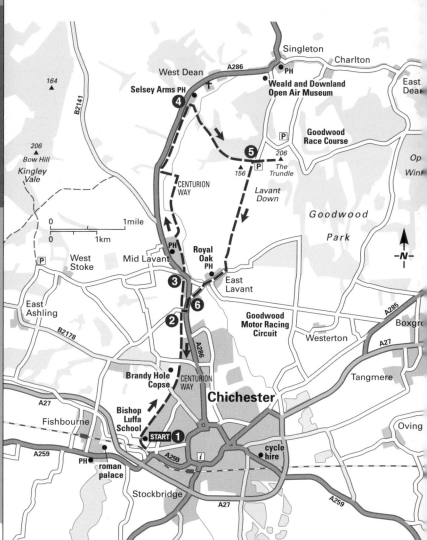

The Selsey Arms

The Selsey Arms is a traditional late 18th-century village pub, well placed for Goodwood, the Weald and Downland Museum and visitors heading to West Dean Gardens. The front bar rooms feature bare boards, horse brasses on beams, dark wood pub tables and chairs, and a friendly, welcoming atmosphere. Daily papers are strewn on a table for customers to read. There's a separate, carpeted restaurant with open fires, beamed ceilings and plain wooden furnishings.

Food

Good-value bar food ranges from sandwiches and ham ploughman's to haddock and chips and home-made steak and kidney pie. A blackboard highlights the bargain two-course lunch and evening extras such as lamb's liver and bacon, red bream, and smoked haddock topped with Welsh rarebit.

Family facilities

Children are welcome inside the pub. The sheltered patio with picnic benches is ideal in fine weather.

Alternative refreshment stops

Try the Royal Oak, East Lavant (on full ride only) or the café at the Weald and Downland Open Air Museum (if visiting).

☛ Where to go from here

The Weald and Downland Open Air Museum (www.wealddown.co.uk) at Singleton, 1 mile (1.6km) east of West Dean, can be reached by driving or cycling along the A286. More than 45 historic buildings, from medieval to Victorian, rescued from south east England, have been rebuilt here. About 0.75 mile (1.2km) along a signposted route from the beginning of this ride or by car via the A259, is Fishbourne Roman Palace (www.sussexpast.co.uk). The largest Roman building north of the Alps, it has outstanding mosaics.

about the pub

The Selsey Arms
West Dean, Chichester
West Sussex PO18 0QX
Tel: 01243 811465

DIRECTIONS: on the A286 at West Dean, between Singleton and Mid Lavant

PARKING: 20

OPEN: daily; all day Saturday and Sunday April to October

FOOD: daily; all day Saturday and Sunday April to October

BREWERY/COMPANY: free house

REAL ALE: Greene King Abbot Ale, Fuller's London Pride, Young's Bitter

From Chichester to Hunston

A fascinating walk combining the ancient treasures of a cathedral city with the delights of the adjacent countryside.

Historic Chichester

A stroll through the quaint streets of Chichester is the best way to appreciate this beautiful city. Chichester's origins date back as far as the late Iron Age, and settled by the Romans in about AD 200. They built the walls and laid out the city plan, which can still be clearly identified.

From the car park you soon find yourself at the heart of Chichester. Make the cathedral your first port of call. This magnificent building includes the site of a shrine to St Richard, Bishop of Chichester in the 13th century, modern tapestries by John Piper and Romanesque stone carvings. Another memorable feature is Graham Sutherland's painting, which depicts Christ appearing to St Mary Magdalen on the first Easter morning.

From the cathedral the walk heads down West Street to the intricately decorated Market Cross, built at the beginning of the 16th century. Situated at the hub of the Roman street plan and distinguished by its flying buttresses, the cross provided shelter for traders. Head up North Street to the Council House, built in 1731 and famous for its huge stone lion and Roman stone. The Latin inscription records the dedication of a temple to Neptune and Minerva. From here it's an easy stroll south to the Pallants.

You then leave the city, by following the Chichester section of the Portsmouth and Arundel Canal out into the countryside and south to Hunston.

the walk

1 Leave the car park, cross the **footbridge** over the Avenue de Chartres and head towards the city centre. Turn right at the city map and then left into South Street. Bear left into **Canon Lane**, just beyond the tourist information centre. Turn right into St Richard's Walk and approach elegant **Chichester Cathedral**.

what to look for

In addition to the remains of the Roman city walls, there is St Mary's Hospital of the Blessed Virgin Mary in St Martin's Square, founded between 1158 and 1170. Originally a hospital, it later became almshouses. Visitors can make an appointment with the guide.

In the nearby Pallants is Pallant House, built by Henry Peckham, a Chichester wine merchant, in 1712. The house is Queen Anne style and each room reflects a particular period of its history.

2h00 · **4.5 MILES** · **7.2 KM** · **LEVEL 123**

MAP: OS Explorer 120 Chichester, South Harting & Selsey

START/FINISH: fee-car park in Avenue de Chartres, Chichester; grid ref: SZ 857044

PATHS: urban walkways, towpath and field paths, 3 stiles

LANDSCAPE: mixture of city streets and open countryside

PUBLIC TOILETS: at car park and elsewhere in Chichester

TOURIST INFORMATION: Chichester tel: 01243 775888

THE PUB: The Spotted Cow, Hunston

🅐 Great care needed when crossing the A27. Suitable for children of all ages.

Getting to the start

Chichester is a city on the south coast between Portsmouth and Bognor Regis. Leave the A27 city bypass at the roundabout where the Witterings are signed to the south and the city centre and railway station to the north. Follow the city centre signs, cross over the railway, then in 200 yards (183m) take the first major turning left – Avenue de Chartres. Pass under the footbridge and exit off the next roundabout into the car park.

Researched and written by:
Nick Channer, David Halford

2 Swing left at the **cloisters**, then left again to keep the stone wall on your left. Make for the West Door and pass the **Bell Tower** to reach West Street. Bear right here. Across the road is a converted church, now a bar. The north face of Chichester Cathedral is clearly seen as you head along West Street. On reaching the **Market Cross**, turn left into North Street and bear right immediately beyond the historic **Council House** into Lion Street.

3 Walk along to **St Martin's Square**, and opposite you at this point is **St Mary's Hospital**. Turn right and pass the Hole in the Wall pub to reach East Street. Glance to the left and you can pick out the **Corn Exchange**. Go straight over into North Pallant and walk along to **Pallant House**. Head straight on into South Pallant and follow the road round to the right, passing **Christ Church** on the left. Turn left at the next junction, make for the traffic lights and continue south into **Southgate**.

4 Cross the railway at **Chichester Station** and then swing left to reach the **canal basin**. Follow the tow path to Poyntz Bridge, dated 1820, and continue to the next bridge which carries the **A27 Chichester bypass**.

Left: Chichester Cathedral
Right: A tapestry and altar inside Chichester Cathedral

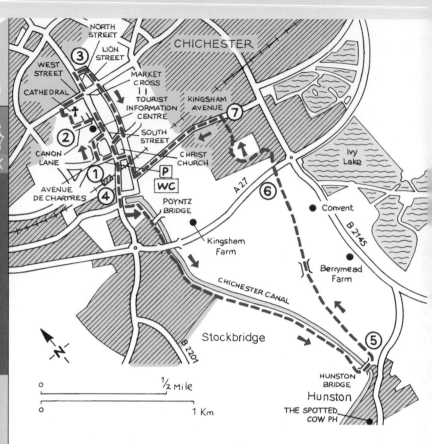

CHICHESTER

NORTH STREET

LION STREET

WEST STREET

CATHEDRAL

MARKET CROSS

TOURIST INFORMATION CENTRE

KINGSHAM AVENUE

CANON LANE

SOUTH STREET

CHRIST CHURCH

P
WC

AVENUE DE CHARTRES

POYNTZ BRIDGE

A 27

Convent

Ivy Lake

B 2145

Kingsham Farm

Berrymead Farm

CHICHESTER CANAL

Stockbridge

B 2201

N

HUNSTON BRIDGE

Hunston

THE SPOTTED COW PH

½ Mile

1 Km

Chichester WEST SUSSEX

25

WALK

Keep going as far as the next footbridge and follow the path to the road. Confusingly this bridge is labelled Poyntz Bridge on OS maps. (Turn right here to reach **The Spotted Cow** pub, about 250 yards/229m along the road on the right.)

5 Bear left for a few steps to a stile by the entrance to a **car park**. Cross into the field. The cathedral's spire can be seen above the city. Keep the **field boundary** on your immediate right and make for a stile. Continue ahead, with a field on your left and follow the path to a small **footbridge** over a ditch and a stile. Follow the edge of the next field, keeping the same direction. Pass by a **broken stile** in the wooded corner and a few steps beyond you reach the **A27**.

6 Cross over with extreme care to join a footpath opposite. Turn left between **two terraces** of houses and follow the tarmac path to the **recreation ground**. Cross to the far side of the green, keeping the cathedral spire more or less straight ahead. Look for **Cherry Orchard Road**, with a post-box and a phone-box on the corner.

7 Turn left at the crossroads into Kingsham Avenue and follow it into Kingsham Road Turn right at the T-junction, cross the **railway line** and, on reaching the one-way system, bear left to cross over at the lights. Bear right into Southgate, then left into **Avenue de Chartres**. The car park is on the left.

The Spotted Cow

about the pub

The Spotted Cow
Selsey Road, Hunston
Chichester, West Sussex PO20 6PD
Tel: 01243 486718
www.thespottedcow.net

DIRECTIONS: village and pub are on the B2145 Selsey road south of Chichester
PARKING: 40
OPEN: daily, all day Friday, Saturday and Sunday
FOOD: daily
BREWERY/COMPANY: free house
REAL ALE: Gales BB and HSB, guest beer
DOGS: welcome on a lead
ROOMS: 2 bedrooms

The Spotted Cow was originally a dairy farm before being converted into a pub in 1955. It's close to the attractions of Chichester harbour and an easy stroll from the city centre via the towpath beside the old canal. Refurbishment in 2000 saw the pub carefully extended to incorporate an old barn, and today it successfully combines the charm and character of a classic country pub (flagstones, heavy beams, open fires) with a modern Mediterranean theme. Upgrading included developing the shaded patio and the sun-trap garden area to the front of the pub. Expect an informal atmosphere, good wines by the glass and local Gales ales on tap.

Food

From an extensive menu you can order snacks and starters such as roast beef and horseradish sandwiches, hearty ploughman's lunches with salad, pickles and crusty bread, fishcakes or scrambled egg and smoked salmon. Main courses include Lancashire hotpot, home-made venison meatballs, fish pie and steak and kidney pie, a range of hand-made sausages, and fresh fish dishes – perhaps sea bass with lemon and coriander.

Family facilities

Families are very welcome and youngsters will find a play area in the garden, a children's menu and reduced price dishes from the blackboard menu. There are baby-changing facilities in the disabled person's toilet.

Alternative refreshment stops

As well as inns and hotels, of which there are many in Chichester, there is Platters restaurant near the Avenue de Chartres car park, and Bishop Bell Rooms close to the cathedral.

☛ Where to go from here

There's plenty to see and do in Chichester, including harbour tours, or head just west of the city to the Roman palace at Fishbourne, with its stunning collection of mosaic floors (www.sussexpast.co.uk).

Meandering in and around Midhurst

A town and country walk which follows the pretty River Rother to the ruins of Cowdray House.

Midhurst

Midhurst's many splendid buildings and a wealth of history add to its charm and character. Look around you on this walk and you'll spot the vivid yellow paintwork of houses owned by the Cowdray Estate. The grounds of Cowdray Park are famous for polo matches. Less well known are the majestic ruins of Cowdray House, seen from the car park at the start of the walk and visited just before the end. The house dates from about 1530 but was largely destroyed by fire in 1793. The still impressive shell survives and you can see around the Great Chamber, the Great Parlour and the Chapel.

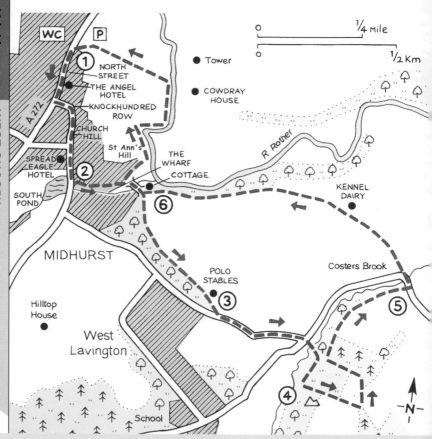

's an easy stroll through the old market own with plenty to see. The famous tile-ung library has been preserved, and the medieval interior is worth a look. Built in he early part of the 16th century, the uilding is thought to have been a torehouse or granary. This part of Midhurst s known as Knockhundred Row.

The road passes the old chemist shop where author H G Wells worked before attending Midhurst Grammar School. In the middle of the street lies the town's war memorial. Follow the road to the imposing Church of St Mary Magdalen and St Denys, which is mostly 19th century.

The walk eventually leaves Midhurst and heads for wooded countryside. It's not long before you are returning to the town, following a path through woods above the Rother. Step between the trees on the right to look down at the river and across to Cowdray House. This vista is one of the highlights of the walk, a moment to savour. The walk finishes by following the Queen's Path, a favourite walk of Elizabeth I.

the walk

1 From the car park turn left and walk along North Street, passing the post office and **The Angel Hotel**. Bear left into

MAP: OS Explorer 120 Chichester, South Harting & Selsey

START/FINISH: free car park by tourist information centre, North Street, Midhurst; grid ref: SZ 886217

PATHS: pavements, field, riverside tracks and country road, 4 stiles

LANDSCAPE: Midhurst town and its beautiful rural setting on the Rother

PUBLIC TOILETS: at car park and elsewhere in Midhurst

TOURIST INFORMATION: Midhurst, tel: 01730 817322

THE PUB: The Angel Hotel, Midhurst

Care needed walking through the town and along the riverside paths. One fairly steep ascent, which can be slippery when wet.

Getting to the start

Midhurst is located on the A272 midway between Petersfield and Petworth. The car park is on North Street as you head out of the town on the A272 towards Petworth.

Researched and written by:
Nick Channer, Peter Toms

The ruins of the Tudor Cowdray House, destroyed by fire in the 18th century

Knockhundred Row, signposted '**South Pond**'. Walk along Church Hill and into South Street, to pass along the side of the historic **Spread Eagle Hotel**.

2 Turn left by South Pond into **The Wharf**. Proceed straight on and at the end of the metalled road turn right over the **bridge**. In 75yds (69m) fork right over a stile and then continue ahead along the field boundary. Cross two stiles in the field corner and follow the path to the right of **polo stables**.

3 Keep left and follow a pleasantly wooded stretch of road. Pass some pretty **cottages,** and on reaching a bend join a bridleway signposted '**Heyshott and Graffham**'. Follow the track as it curves to the right.

4 Veer left just before the entrance to a house and follow the **waymarked bridleway** as it climbs steeply through the trees. Drop down the slope passing between woodland glades and carpets of bracken, to a **waymarked path junction**. Turn left to join a **sandy track**. Keep left at the fork and follow the track as it curves left, then right.

5 On reaching the road, turn left. When it bends left by some gates, go straight on along the bridleway towards **Kennel Dairy**. Continue straight on between **stable blocks**

what to look for

South Pond is one of Midhurst's most popular attractions. Donated to the town by Lord Cowdray in 1957, the pond is part of a tributary of the Rother. Mute swans, Canada geese and mallards can be seen here. A path running alongside South Pond was opened in 1977 to mark the Queen's Silver Jubilee.

Have a look at St Ann's Hill, just off the route of the walk, above the River Rother. This natural mound was once the site of a fortified Norman castle, though all that remains of it today are a few stones on this grassy knoll. Information panels explain the history of the site in some detail.

and through two gates. When the track enters a field, go through the gate to the right of it, following the path as it runs just inside the **woodland**.

6 Continue along to the junction, forming part of the outward leg of the walk, turn right and retrace your steps over the **bridge**. Bear half-right to join the path alongside the **River Rother** (where the path follows the river to the right a path sharp left leads up to the ruins on St Ann's Hill). Go through a kissing gate, turn left and make for a bridge which provides access to **Cowdray House**. After visiting the house, go straight ahead along the **causeway path** to return to the car park.

Above: South Pond is on the route of the walk

The Angel Hotel

An elegant Georgian façade disguises the history of this much-extended coaching inn, which actually dates from the 16th century. The Angel is virtually plumb in the town centre, with the front of the hotel overlooking the bustling main street, while to the rear the very beautiful gardens, which include a Victorian walled garden, give way to peaceful meadowland and the dramatic ruins of Cowdray Castle. Public areas are largely centred around the Halo bar/brasserie at the front of the hotel, and the smart restaurant and function areas to the rear. Watch the world go by from the informal bar over coffee or a decent light lunch, or treat the family to afternoon tea on warmer days in the garden, a civilised end to this short walk.

Food

Options from the brasserie menu include Moroccan-spiced lamb burger, Thai fishcakes with hot dipping sauce, roast monkfish with a herb risotto, and honey-roast duck breast with cabbage, bacon and blackcurrant jus. Good lighter lunchtime snacks and meals.

Family facilities

Children are welcome throughout the hotel and smaller portions from the main menu can be provided. Other facilities include high chairs and warming of baby food.

Alternative refreshment stops

The aptly named Chukkas in Midhurst Walk, the Coffee Pot in Knockhundred Row and Ye Olde Tea Shoppe in North Street all offer tea, coffee and lunches.

☞ Where to go from here

Some of the best paintings in the National Trust's collection are displayed at Petworth House, a 17th-century mansion set in a 700-acre (284ha) deer park, east of Midhurst on the A272 (www.nationaltrust.org.uk).

about the pub

The Angel Hotel
North Street, Midhurst
West Sussex GU29 9DN
Tel: 01730 812421
www. theangelmidhurst.co.uk

DIRECTIONS: in the centre of the town	
PARKING: 75	
OPEN: daily, all day	
FOOD: daily	
BREWERY/COMPANY: free house	
REAL ALE: Gales Best and HSB	
DOGS: welcome in the lounge area and garden	
ROOMS: 28 en suite	

From Goodwood to Charlton and beyond

WALK

One of Britain's top racecourses lies beside this woodland walk, which includes an optional spur to the Weald and Downland Open Air Museum.

Goodwood

WEST SUSSEX

Glorious Goodwood

Think of horse racing on the South Downs and you immediately think of Goodwood, one of Britain's loveliest and most famous racecourses. The course rises and falls around a natural amphitheatre, with the horses dashing along the ridge to create one of the greatest spectacles in the racing world. For one week every summer it becomes 'Glorious Goodwood' when thousands of racegoers travel to Sussex to attend one of the most prestigious events of the sporting and social calendar. According to *The Times*, Goodwood is 'the place to be and to be seen'.

The course opened in 1801 after the Duke of Richmond donated Goodwood Park to establish a track where members of the Goodwood Hunt Club and officers of the Sussex Militia could attend meetings.

The walk begins at Goodwood Country Park, a popular amenity area characterised by woodland and grassy downland, and initially follows part of the Monarch's Way through extensive woodland, down to the village of East Dean. Along the road is neighbouring Charlton, famous for the Charlton Hunt, established in the 18th century. The hunt's most memorable chase took place on 28th January 1738, beginning before eight that morning and not finishing until nearly six that evening.

Many of those taking part were from the elite upper ranks of society and for ten hours a fox led them a merry dance in the surrounding fields and woods.

If time allows (allow at least 3 hours – 2 miles/3.2km there and back plus plenty to see on site), you can extend the walk at this point and visit the outstanding Weald & Downland Open Air Museum, with its unusual collection of traditional country homes and workplaces.

The grand ivy-covered façade of 18th-century Goodwood House

The walk

1 Make for the western end of Counter's Gate car park and look for a **footpath sign** by an opening leading out to the road. Cross over to a junction of two clear tracks, with a path on the right. Follow the right-hand track, signposted 'public footpath' and part of the **Monarch's Way**, to a gate and stile. Continue past hazel thickets to the next gate and stile, then cross a clearing in the woods.

2 Follow the gently curving path to the right over the grassy, plant-strewn ground and down between trees to reach a **gateway**. The village of **East Dean** can be seen nestling down below. Head diagonally right down the steep field slope to a stile in the corner.

3 Cross into the adjacent field and keep to the right of the boundary fence to a **second stile** leading out to the road. Bear left and walk down into East Dean, passing **Manor Farm**.

4 Turn left at the junction, signed to Singleton (or right, signed to Petworth, to visit the **Star & Garter Inn**), and follow the road towards Charlton. On reaching the village, walk on past **The Fox Goes Free** pub and the Woodstock House Hotel, then take the road left, signed to **Goodwood**.

Titchfield's 16th-century Market Hall and two 15th-century buildings at the Weald and Downland Open Air Museum

1h30 — **5 MILES** — **8 KM** — **LEVEL 1** 2 3

SHORTER ALTERNATIVE ROUTE

1h30 — **3.5 MILES** — **5.7 KM** — **LEVEL 1** 2 3

MAP: OS Explorers 120 Chichester, South Harting & Selsey, 121 Arundel & Pulborough
START/FINISH: Counter's Gate free car park and picnic area, Goodwood Country Park; or large free car park opposite racecourse; grid ref: TQ 897113 (on Explorer 120)
PATHS: woodland tracks and field paths, section of Monarch's Way and one lengthy stretch of quiet road, 4 stiles
LANDSCAPE: mixture of dense woodland and scenic downland
PUBLIC TOILETS: only if visiting the Weald & Downland Museum
TOURIST INFORMATION: Chichester, tel: 01243 775888
THE PUB: The Fox Goes Free, Charlton
🛈 Take extra care on the road linking East Dean and Charlton. One steep climb back to the Country Park

Getting to the start

Goodwood Racecourse and Country Park lie between Midhurst and Chichester, clearly signed on a minor road between the A286 and the A185.

Researched and written by:
Nick Channer, Peter Toms

WALK

Goodwood · WEST SUSSEX

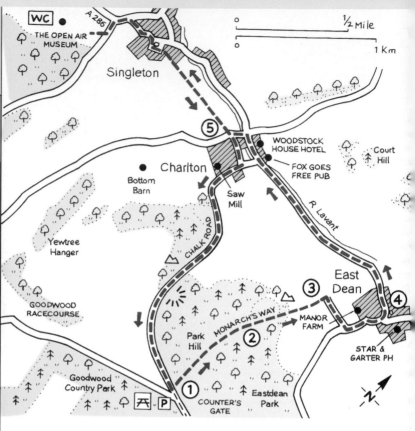

5 In 100yds (91m) take the lane left (or the footpath right and straight across fields to visit the **Weald & Downland Museum** at Singleton, returning to this stile by the same route). In a further 100yds (91m), fork left and turn right by the **war memorial**, dedicated to fallen comrades of the Sussex Yeomanry in both world wars. Follow **Chalk Road**, which dwindles to a track on the outskirts of Charlton. Once clear of the village, go through a gate, the track climbing steadily between the trees. On the left are glimpses of a glorious rolling landscape, while to the right Goodwood's superbly set **racecourse** edges into view between the trees. Follow the track all the way to the road and cross over to **Counter's Gate car park**.

what to look for

The village of East Dean, with its pond and ancient cottages of Sussex flint, is one of the prettiest in the area. For many years it was a thriving centre for hurdlemaking, and before World War One seven craftsmen operated here. The Weald and Downland Open Air Museum is set in 50 acres (20ha) of lovely Sussex countryside and offers a fascinating collection of over 40 regional historic buildings which have been saved from destruction, painstakingly restored and rebuilt in their original form. You can discover Victorian labourers' cottages, visit a recreated Tudor farmstead and explore ancient building techniques in the museum's hands-on gallery (www.wealddown.co.uk).

The Fox Goes Free

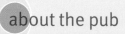

Built in 1558, the pub was a favoured hunting lodge of William III. More recently, it hosted the first Women's Institute meeting in 1915. The lovely old brick-and-flint building nestles in unspoilt rolling South Downs countryside and has a splendid flint-walled rear garden with apple trees, rustic benches, a barbecue area, and views across sheep-grazed pastures. Inside, the pub exudes charm and character with two huge fireplaces, a low-beamed ceiling, high-backed wooden settles and worn brick floors. On handpump you'll find local ale from Ballards and Arundel breweries, and there are eight wines available by the glass. Comfortable overnight accommodation is offered – very handy for Goodwood Races.

Food

The menu marries traditional and modern styles, and typical dishes include ham, egg and chips, rump of lamb, calf's liver and bacon, steak and kidney pie, local game and fresh fish. Sandwiches, filled baguettes and ploughman's lunches are available at lunchtime.

Family facilities

Children are welcome inside, and families can enjoy the spacious garden on fine summer days. Smaller portions of main dishes are available for children.

about the pub

The Fox Goes Free
Charlton, Goodwood, Chichester
West Sussex PO18 0HU
Tel: 01243 811461

DIRECTIONS: Charlton and the pub are signposted 1 mile (1.6km) off the A286 Chichester to Midhurst road at Singleton

PARKING: 6

OPEN: daily, all day

FOOD: daily, all day Saturday and Sunday

BREWERY/COMPANY: free house

REAL ALE: Ballards Best, Timothy Taylor Landlord, Arundel Best, Fox Bitter, guest beer

DOGS: welcome in the bar and garden

ROOMS: 5 en suite

Alternative refreshment stops

The Star and Garter at East Dean also offers a good range of meals and snacks. There is a café at the Weald & Downland Museum.

☞ Where to go from here

Goodwood House (www.goodwood.co.uk) has State Apartments and paintings by Van Dyck, Reynolds, Stubbs and Canaletto.

Around the Arun Valley from Arundel

WALK

Follow the River Arun to Arundel Park and then tour this handsome Sussex town.

Arundel

Arundel has rows of elegant Georgian and Victorian buildings, fine shops and a picturesque riverside setting, but the best attraction is surely the magnificent castle. Driving along the A27 to the south of Arundel, the great battlemented castle can be seen standing guard over the town, dwarfing all other buildings in sight.

There has been a castle here since the 11th century, though most of the present structure is Victorian. Arundel Castle has been the principal home of the Dukes of Norfolk since the 16th century. During the Civil War Parliamentary forces attacked the castle. However, it was extensively rebuilt and restored in the 18th and 19th centuries. Within its great walls lies a treasure trove of sumptuous riches.

The walk starts down by the River Arun and from here there are teasing glimpses of the castle, but it is not until you have

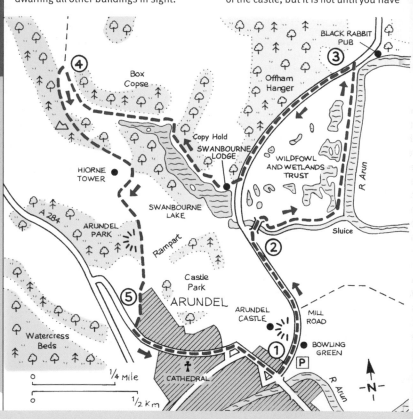

what to look for

Climbing up from Arundel Park brings you to Hiorne Tower, a remote but beautifully situated folly. Triangular in shape and newly restored, the folly was built by Francis Hiorne in an effort to ingratiate himself with the then Duke of Norfolk so that he might work on the restoration of Arundel Castle. The duke agreed to engage him but Hiorne died before he could begin work.

The Wildfowl and Wetlands Trust Conservation Centre, which is directly on the route of the walk, has many attractions to divert your attention. Ducks, geese and swans from all over the world make their home here and the boardwalk enables you to explore one of the largest reed beds in Sussex.

almost finished the walk that you reach its main entrance. Following the riverbank through the tranquil Arun valley, the walk reaches Arundel Park. Swanbourne Lake, a great attraction for young children, is by the entrance to the park, but beyond here the park assumes a different character. Rolling hills and tree-clad slopes crowd in and only occasional walkers will be seen in these more remote surroundings. You may feel isolated but you are soon back in Arundel's busy streets. Pass the huge cathedral, built in 1870, and head to the castle entrance. Walk down the High Street, said to be the steepest in England, and by the bridge you can see the remains of the Blackfriars monastery, dissolved in 1546 by Henry VIII.

Walking through an open stretch on the route

2h00 — **3.25 MILES** — **5.3 KM** — **LEVEL 1 2 3**

WALK

Arun Valley

WEST SUSSEX

MAP: OS Explorer 121 Arundel & Pulborough

START/FINISH: fee-paying car park, Mill Road, Arundel; grid ref: TQ 020071

PATHS: riverside and parkland paths, some road walking, 2 stiles

LANDSCAPE: valley, rolling parkland and town

PUBLIC TOILETS: Arundel town centre and Swanbourne Lake

TOURIST INFORMATION: Arundel, tel: 01903 882268

THE PUB: Black Rabbit, Offham

🛈 Section of road with no pavement (generally light traffic). Arundel Park is closed annually on 24 March. Dogs are not permitted in Arundel Park

Getting to the start

Arundel is located just off the A27 between Chichester and Worthing, 10 miles (16.1km) east of Chichester. If heading west on the A27, exit for the town centre at the first roundabout. Cross the River Arun and turn right into Mill Road. The car park is 100yds (91m) along on the right.

Researched and written by:
Nick Channer, David Halford

Swans in the Wildfowl and Wetlands Trust reserve at Arundel

the walk

1 From the car park in Mill Road, turn right and walk along the tree-lined pavement. Pass the **bowling green** and a glance to your left will reveal a dramatic view of Arundel Castle with its imposing battlements.

2 Follow the road to the elegant stone bridge, cross over via a **footbridge** and turn right. Ignore the path left, and follow the riverside path, partly shaded by overhanging trees. Emerging from the cover, the path cuts across lush, low-lying ground to reach the western bank of the **Arun**. Turn left and walk beside the reed-fringed river to the **Black Rabbit pub**, which can be seen standing out against a curtain of trees.

3 From the Black Rabbit, follow the minor road in a roughly westerly direction back towards Arundel, passing the entrance to the **Wildfowl and Wetlands Trust**. Make for the gate leading into Arundel Park and follow the path beside **Swanbourne Lake**.

Eventually the lake fades from view as the walk reaches deeper into the park. Ignore a turning branching off to the left, just before a **gate and stile**, and follow the path as it curves gently to the right.

4 Turn sharply to the left at the next **waymarked junction** and begin a fairly steep ascent, with the footpath through the park seen curving away down to the left, back towards the **lake**. This stretch of the walk offers fine views over Arundel Park. Pass through a gate with a stile on the left, then bear immediately right up the bank. Cross the grass, following the waymarks and keeping to the left of **Hiorne Tower**. On reaching a driveway, turn left and walk down to **Park Lodge**. Keep to the right by the private drive and make for the road.

5 Turn left, pass **Arundel Cathedral** and bear left at the road junction by the entrance to Arundel Castle. Go down the hill, back into the centre of Arundel. You'll find **Mill Road** at the bottom of the High Street.

Black Rabbit

This uniquely named pub is popular with walkers and tourists visiting Arundel and the nearby Wildfowl and Wetlands Trust reserve. It stands right beside the River Arun, and from its riverside terrace you can relax and enjoy excellent views down the river to Arundel's magnificent castle. Once a fashionable watering hole for the Edwardians, it retains the appearance of being an elegant riverside summer house, and what were once probably old boat sheds now form part of the pub's main dining area. Wood floors, traditional furnishings and a winter log fire are features of the long main bar. Seating is also provided under the attractive front verandah, which makes a real picture in summer with colourful hanging baskets and tubs.

Food
Sandwiches, filled baguettes and a choice of ploughman's lunches are listed on the blackboard in the bar. From the printed menu you can sample honey-roast ham, egg and chips, steak and Tanglefoot pie, warm chicken and bacon salad and garlic chicken, and round off with apple and blackberry crumble.

Family facilities
Children are most welcome, and although a 'junior menu' is available, children are encouraged to be adventurous and try a starter or smaller portions from the main menu. To keep youngsters away from the river there is a play area beside the car park.

Alternative refreshment stops
Arundel has a good choice of places to eat and drink. The Wildfowl and Wetlands Trust offers a café by the water's edge, and there is a picnic site by Swanbourne Lake.

☛ Where to go from here
Arundel Museum and Heritage Centre illustrates the town's colourful and lively past with a series of fascinating exhibits and photographs, providing a unique glimpse into the development of the town and the lives of its people.

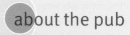

about the pub

Black Rabbit
Offham, Arundel
West Sussex BN18 9PB
Tel: 01903 882828

DIRECTIONS: continue along Mill Road from Arundel town centre for Offham	
PARKING: 180	
OPEN: daily, all day	
FOOD: daily, all day	
BREWERY/COMPANY: Hall and Woodhouse Brewery	
REAL ALE: King & Barnes Bitter, Badger Best, Tanglefoot and Fursty Ferret	
DOGS: allowed in part of the bar and garden	

A downland ramble at Amberley

Re-create the past with a visit to a working museum before climbing high on to the Downs.

Amberley Working Museum

Amberley is a charming, tranquil village with a history going back to medieval times and was the summer residence of the Bishops of Chichester. It may sound strange, but this invigorating downland walk begins where reality meets nostalgia. By visiting an old chalk quarry at the start of the route, you have the chance to forget – however briefly – the hurly-burly of the modern world, step into the past and recall a cherished way of life that has long vanished.

Amberley Working Museum is well worth a visit (www.amberleymuseum.co.uk). The open-air museum, which covers 36 acres (15ha) of a long-disused chalk pit in the Arun Valley, opened in 1979. Originally called the Chalk Pits Museum, its objective is to illustrate how the traditional industries of south east England evolved and developed during the 19th and 20th centuries. And it is very successful – few museums thrill and excite adults and children alike as much as this one does. To prove it, there are almost 100,000 visitors a year.

Visit the bus garage and the signwriter's workshop, the locomotive shed, the village blacksmith's, stop at the telephone exchange or discover the wheelwright's shop. You may meet craftspeople from the museum's resident team exercising ancient skills. Using traditional materials and tools, they produce a choice of fine wares which enables them to earn a living and keep their trade thriving. Elsewhere, exhibits

are conserved and demonstrated by volunteers, many of whom have acquired a lifetime's experience in their trade.

One of the highlights of a visit to the Amberley Working Museum is a trip around the site on board a vintage bus, or perhaps a tour on the narrow gauge railway. The train ride takes visitors between Amberley and Brockham stations and yet never leaves the museum site! When you finally leave the museum follow the River Arun and begin the gradual climb into the hills. Up here, with its wide open skies and far-ranging views, you can feel the bracing wind in your face as you explore some of the loneliest tracts of downland in Sussex.

the walk

1 Turn left out of the car park and pass under the **railway bridge**. Begin to cross the road bridge spanning the River Arun and then bear left at the **footpath sign** to a stile by a galvanised gate. Once over it, cross the **watermeadows** to the next stile, and a few paces beyond it you reach a footpath sign. Bear left here.

2 Follow the path between trees, turn right on reaching a lane and pass **Sloe Cottage**. Turn left just beyond a caravan site to join a bridleway. Follow the path as it runs above the **camping ground** until it meets a track with a bridleway sign. Cross the track here and join a rough lane.

3 Stay on the lane as it climbs gradually. The Arun can be seen below, threading its way through the valley. Pass some **ruined farm outbuildings** and keep ahead,

Old traction engines at Amberley Working Museum

2h00 — **5.5 MILES** — **8.8 KM** — **LEVEL 2**

MAP: OS Explorer 121 Arundel & Pulborough

START/FINISH: Amberley Working Museum car park, by Amberley Station. Visit the museum, then leave your car here while on the walk, by kind permission of the museum management; grid ref: TQ 026117

PATHS: riverside paths, downland tracks and some roads, 5 stiles

LANDSCAPE: Arun Valley and downland

PUBLIC TOILETS: Amberley Museum

TOURIST INFORMATION: Arundel, tel: 01903 882268

THE PUB: The Bridge Inn, Houghton Bridge
🚸 Short section beside and crossing busy road; suitable for children of all ages.

Getting to the start

Amberley Working Museum is signed off the B2139, between Arundel and Storrington. Note that the car park is not available on days when special events are taking place at the museum, and also that it is locked at around 6pm.

Researched and written by:
Nick Channer, David Halford

he lane dwindling to a track along this tretch. Veer left at the fork and follow the **aymarked public right of way**. Head for a ignposted crossroads and take the left-and **public bridleway**.

4 Walk down the **chalk track**, pass through a gate and continue the steep escent. Look for two gates down below, set ome distance apart. Cross to the right-and gate and a reassuring bridleway sign s seen here. Follow the bridleway as it ends left, climbing steeply towards **Downs arm**. Keep a fence on the left and follow the ridleway as it merges with a wide track.

5 Keep left at the next junction and follow the **South Downs Way** towards the ntrance to **Downs Farm**. Veer to the right f the gateway and join a narrow footpath

Amberley   WEST SUSSEX

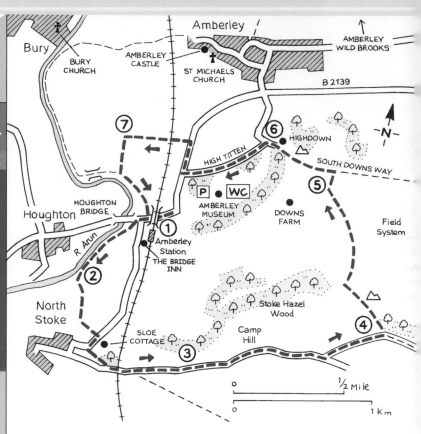

Amberley

AMBERLEY WILD BROOKS

Bury

BURY CHURCH

AMBERLEY CASTLE

St MICHAELS CHURCH

B 2139

⑦

HIGH TITTEN

⑥ **HIGHDOWN**

SOUTH DOWNS WAY

-N-

P ● WC

AMBERLEY MUSEUM

DOWNS FARM

Field System

⑤

HOUGHTON BRIDGE

Houghton

R. Arun

① **Amberley Station**
THE BRIDGE INN

②

North Stoke

SLOE COTTAGE

③

Stoke Hazel Wood

Camp Hill

④

½ Mile

1 Km

which begins a steep descent. Drop down the slope until you reach a tarmac lane and turn right. On the right-hand side is a prominent house called **Highdown**.

6 Veer left at the fork and follow a lane called **High Titten** between trees and hedgerows. The attractions of **Amberley Working Museum** can be spotted at intervals along this stretch. On reaching the road junction, turn right and follow the tarmac path parallel to the road. Turn left at the **South Downs Way sign** and follow the concrete track over the railway line to a **galvanised gate**.

7 Turn left here and follow the bridleway to the bank of the River Arun. Swing left

veering slightly away from the **riverbank**, t[…] join a drive and then turn left at the road. Cross over and turn right to return to Amberley Working Museum and its car par[…]

what to look for

A church at North Stoke, just off the route, is mentioned in the Domesday Book, though nothing here is earlier than the 13th century. The windows in both transepts have some of the most striking early tracery in southern England. From the higher ground, above North Stoke, look across the Arun Valley to the 'Alpine' spire of the church at South Stoke. On a good day you might pick out distant Arundel Castle.

he Bridge Inn

st two minutes walk from Amberley
orking Museum and the start/finish of
e walk, the Bridge Inn dates from 1650
nd enjoys a super position close to the
ver Arun. Make the most of the sunny
rrace and the lovely views in summer,
hile on cooler days you can retreat inside
e Grade II listed building and relax in the
ttractive and comfortable open-plan bar
nd adjoining dining areas. Open log
res, Harveys Sussex Bitter on handpump
nd a welcoming atmosphere enhance the
harm of The Bridge.

about the pub

The Bridge Inn
Houghton Bridge, Amberley
West Sussex BN18 9LR
Tel: 01798 831619

DIRECTIONS: Houghton lies west of
Amberley on the B2139

PARKING: 16

OPEN: daily, all day Friday, Saturday and
Sunday

FOOD: no food Monday evening

BREWERY/COMPANY: Enterprise Inns

REAL ALE: Harveys Sussex, Fuller's London
Pride, guest beer

DOGS: welcome in the bar and garden

Family facilities
Families are welcome inside, and young
children have their own menu.

Alternative refreshment stops
There is also a tea room at Houghton
Bridge, and a restaurant at the Amberley
Working Museum.

☛ Where to go from here
Head west for a few miles to visit Bignor
Roman Villa and Museum, the remains of
a grand house with the longest Roman
mosaic (82ft/25m) in Britain (www.
romansinsussex.co.uk).

ood
mong the popular dishes are steak, Stilton
nd mushroom pie, loin of pork with
reamed horseradish and parsnip, sea bass
rilled with rosemary, Sussex sausages and
nash, fresh tuna with mango and ginger
hutney, and traditional roast beef on
Sunday. Snacks include ploughman's
unches and mussels cooked in garlic,
erbs, cream and white wine, served
with crusty bread.

Amberley and Bignor Roman Villa

A tour of sandy forests and heathland, and thatched villages snuggling below the South Downs.

Amberley and Bignor

The little knot of streets in Amberley is worth exploring house by house: an extraordinary number of them are thatched or half-timbered. At the start or finish of the ride, follow the no-through road past the church to reach the outer wall of the medieval castle. It is now a hotel and not open to the public, but is worth a look for its marvellous position, brooding over the marshy meadow known as Amberley Wild

Brooks, a rich haunt of birdlife, including teal and Bewick swans.

As you approach Bignor Roman Villa, all you see is a series of strange thatched huts. These shelter what is one of the fine Roman villas ever discovered in Britain. It was found in 1811 by Joseph Tupper who was ploughing the land here when he unearthed a magnificent mosaic floor depicting Ganymede's abduction by an eagle. It was soon realised how important this mostly 4th century AD building was, ar the farmer made it a tourist attraction, erecting these shelters. Many Roman villa were built in locations with a beautiful vie and Bignor is no exception.

Amberley

WEST SUSSEX

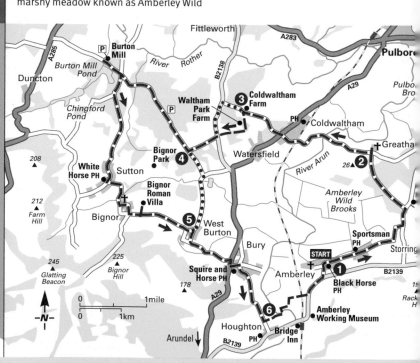

the ride

1 With The Black Horse on your right and the White House on your left follow the road out of Amberley. Past the **Sportsman pub**, turn left at a T-junction (signposted Greatham). By a building on the left you will see some **sandstone crags** away to the left, an inviting feature for children to clamber up. Turn left at the next junction, signposted Greatham. (If you carry on a short way towards Wiggonholt you will reach the lodge on the right at the edge of Parham Park; from here a ten-minute walk into the estate gives you a good distant view of the grand Elizabethan house.)

2 At the next junction, turn left to **Coldwaltham**, but first detour ahead along a track to **Greatham church** (soon reached via a gate on the right). This is a lovely, unspoilt church with no electricity – it's lit by oil lamps – and with ancient beam structures known as kingposts supporting the roof. The route soon crosses **Greatham Bridge**, with its ten rather wonky arches (a footpath on the near side gives access to the river bank and a lovely view). Wheel across the A29 carefully and take the road ahead signposted **Fittleworth**.

3 After **Coldwaltham Farm** on the right, turn left on a farm road towards **Waltham Park Farm** (if you prefer to avoid the off-road section, do not turn off here; instead carry on to the B2138, turn left then take the first right, signposted Bignor). Fork left at the farm, down an eroded **rocky track**, and turn right at the bottom on a **signposted bridleway** (avoiding the

---

| 3h00 | 15 MILES | 24.1 KM | LEVEL 1 2 3 |

SHORTER ALTERNATIVE ROUTE

| 2h15 | 11 MILES | 17.7 KM | LEVEL 1 2 3 |

30

CYCLE

MAP: OS Explorer 121 Arundel and Pulborough
START/FINISH: The Black Horse, Amberley village centre; grid ref: TQ 030132
TRAILS/TRACKS: nearly all on quiet roads, with a short section over fields and along well-drained but very sandy tracks; a road alternative is provided
LANDSCAPE: woodland, wetland, parkland, farmland and views of the South Downs
PUBLIC TOILETS: none on route
TOURIST INFORMATION: Arundel, tel: 01903 882268
CYCLE HIRE: City Cycles, 44 Bognor Road, Chichester, West Sussex, tel: 01243 539992
THE PUB: The Black Horse, Amberley
🅕 Dismount to cross the A29. The off-road section at Point **3** avoids the B2138, which can be busy, but you will have to push your bike along a soft, sandy path. The full ride has two steep hills

Amberley   WEST SUSSEX

Getting to the start

Turn off the B2139 between Storrington and the A29 at a sign for Amberley and the Black Horse. Park on roadside.

Why do this cycle ride?

From the thatched village of Amberley, the route heads along quiet lanes looking up to the South Downs, before passing silent country estates, timber-framed cottages and the entrance to Bignor Roman Villa. You might spot birds over the wetland of Amberley Wild Brooks.

Researched and written by: Tim Locke

signposted footpath just before). The route is sandy and you will have to push most of the way. Cross the B2138, taking the road ahead signposted Bignor.

Previous page: Detail from a mosaic found at the Roman Villa at Bignor
Below: A large cottage in Amberley

4 For the short route turn left in front of the gates to **Bignor Park** to follow signs for **Bignor Roman Villa**; keep right at the first junction and rejoin the main route in West Burton. For the full route, turn right at the gates. Pass a large heath – **Lord's Piece** – grazed by ponies on the left; this is the last site in Britain where you can find field crickets. At the top, keep left towards **Duncton**. At the next junction go straight ahead to **Burton Pond**, which was created for the long-vanished iron industry and which once powered Burton Mill (occasionally open in summer). Here you may spot kingfishers, bitterns and great crested grebes, and there's a nature trail that skirts the pond. Return to the junction and turn right towards **Sutton**. Turn left in Sutton, by the **White Horse pub**, following signs to Bignor, and pass a wonderful

thatched, half-timbered 15th-century house called Yeoman's House. After Bignor church continue to Bignor Roman Villa, then carry on to West Burton.

5 In West Burton take the road signposted to Bury, crossing the **A29** by the traffic island and taking the road opposite and to the right to **Bury**. Turn right in the village, towards **Houghton**.

6 After 1 mile (1.6km) turn left on the **South Downs Way** (marked with blue arrows) and follow the waymarkers across two fields, turning right on the river bank, over the **river bridge** and right on the other side, then left. At the **B2139**, turn left and take the first road on the left back into **Amberley**.

The Black Horse

The Black Horse is a lovely old pub at the heart of this beautiful South Downs village, often called the 'Pearl of Sussex'. One of several knocked-through cottages, it has been nicely revamped, with flagstones, dark red walls, log fires, old pictures and prints on the walls, and heavy beams hung with sheep bells and shepherds tools, donated by the last shepherd to have a flock on the South Downs.

Food

Good traditional bar food is served throughout the pub. Choices include sandwiches (with salad and chips), ploughman's lunches, lasagne, steak and ale pie and home-made curries. Evening dishes may include rack of lamb and fillet steak with tiger prawns.

about the pub

The Black Horse
High Street, Amberley
West Sussex BN18 9LR
Tel: 01798 831552

DIRECTIONS: at the north end of the village: from the B2139, drive into Amberley keeping right at the junction; the pub is on the next corner

PARKING: street parking only

OPEN: daily; all day

FOOD: daily; all day Sunday

BREWERY/COMPANY: Pubmaster

REAL ALE: Greene King IPA, Charles Wells Bombardier

Family facilities

Children over the age of six are allowed in the bar and restaurant if they are well behaved and eating with their parents. On fine days head for the lovely walled garden.

Alternative refreshment stops

Try the Sportsman, just east of Amberley, the White Horse in Sutton or the Squire and Horse on the A29 at Bury. Burton Mill sometimes serves teas in high summer (tel: 01798 869575 to check first). There is also Houghton Bridge Riverside Tea Garden and Restaurant and The Bridge Inn just off the route near Amberley Working Museum and by the B2139 river bridge.

☞ Where to go from here

Set in a disused chalk pit Amberley Working Museum (www.amberleymuseum.co.uk) is an open-air museum giving an absorbing look at the industrial heritage of the south east, and featuring transport, electricity, telecommunications, industries such as printing, a wheelwright's and resident craftspeople – among them a blacksmith and a clay-pipe maker. Visit the Roman Villa at Bignor along the route (www. romansinsussex.co.uk).

A circuit of Devil's Dyke by Poynings

A fine walk with glimpses over the most famous of all the dry chalk valleys.

Devil's Dyke

Sussex is rich in legend and folklore, and the Devil and his fiendish works crop up all over the county. The local landmark of Devil's Dyke blends the natural beauty of the South Downs with the mystery and originality of ancient mythology.

Devil's Dyke is a geological quirk – a spectacular, steep-sided downland combe or cleft 300ft (91m) deep and half a mile (800m) long. It was probably cut by glacial meltwaters in the Ice Age. Rising to over 600ft (180m), views from this beauty spot stretch for miles in all directions. Artist John Constable described this view as the grandest in the world.

Devil's Dyke has long been a tourist honey pot. During the Victorian era and in the early part of the 20th century, the place was akin to a bustling theme park, with a cable car crossing the valley and a steam railway coming up from Brighton. On Whit Monday 1893 a staggering 30,000 people visited the area. In 1928 HRH the Duke of York dedicated the Dyke Estate for the use of the public forever, and in fine weather it can seem just as crowded as it was in Queen Victoria's day. With the car park full and the surrounding slopes busy with people, Devil's Dyke assumes the feel of a seaside resort at the height of the season. Hang gliders swoop over the grassy downland like pterodactyls, and kite flyers spill from their cars. The views more than make up for all the visitors, and away from the chalk slopes and the car park the walk heads for more peaceful surroundings.

the walk

1 From the Summer Down car park go through the kissing gate and veer right. Join the **South Downs Way** and follow it alongside lines of trees. Soon the path curves left and drops down to the road. Part company with the South Downs Way at this point, as it crosses over to join the **private road** to Saddlescombe, and follow the verge for about 75yds (69m). Bear left at the footpath sign and drop down the bank to a stile.

2 Follow the line of the tarmac lane as it curves right to reach a **waymark**. Leave the lane and walk ahead alongside **power lines**, keeping the line of trees and bushes on the right. Look for a narrow path disappearing into the vegetation and make for a stile. Drop down some steps into the woods and turn right at a **junction** with a bridleway. Take the path running off half-left and follow it between fields and a wooded dell. Pass over a stile and continue to a stile in the left boundary. Cross a footbridge to a further stile and now turn right towards **Poynings**.

3 Head for a gate and footpath sign and turn left at the road. Follow the parallel path along to the **Royal Oak** and then continue to **Dyke Lane** on the left. There is a **memorial stone** here to George Stephen Cave Cuttress, a resident of Poynings for over 50 years, erected by his widow. Follow the tarmac bridleway and soon it narrows to a path. On reaching the fork, by a National Trust sign for **Devil's Dyke**, veer right and begin climbing the steps.

The South Downs seen from Devil's Dyke

1h30 — **3 MILES** — **4.8 KM** — **LEVEL 1 2 3**

WALK

MAP: OS Explorer 122 South Downs Way: Steyning to Newhaven

START/FINISH: free car park, Summer Down; grid ref: TQ 268112

PATHS: field and woodland paths, 6 stiles

LANDSCAPE: chalk grassland, steep escarpment and woodland

PUBLIC TOILETS: by Devil's Dyke pub

TOURIST INFORMATION: Brighton, tel: 0906 711 2255

THE PUB: Royal Oak, Poynings

🛑 Steep steps up the South Downs. Suitable for fitter, older children.

Getting to the start

Poynings is north of Brighton, west of the A23. Take the A281 for Henfield, then turn left for Poynings. Turn left in front of the church, then at the next T-junction, turn right. Follow this road for about 1 mile (1.6km) and turn right, signposted 'Dyke'. The car park is on the right after about 500yds (457m).

Researched and written by:
Nick Channer, David Halford

Devil's Dyke

EAST SUSSEX

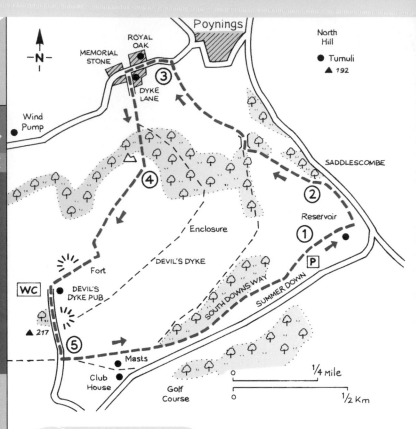

what to look for

Devil's Dyke consists of 183 acres (74ha) of open downland which is home to all manner of flora and fauna, including horseshoe vetch, the Pride of Sussex flower and the common spotted orchid. The adonis blue butterfly also inhabits the area. The Dyke lies within the South Downs Area of Outstanding Natural Beauty and is a designated Site of Special Scientific Interest (SSSI).

Take a stroll through the village of Poynings, pronounced 'Punnings' locally. The village takes its name from the Poynages family, which held the manor here during the Middle Ages. Michael de Poynages, a 14th-century lord of the manor, left two hundred marcs (£2,400) in his will towards the building of the Church of Holy Trinity.

4 Follow the path up to a gate and continue up the **stairs**. From the higher ground there are breathtaking views to the north and west. Make for a **kissing gate** and head up the slope towards the inn. Keep the **Devil's Dyke pub** on your left and take the road round to the left, passing a bridleway on the left. Follow the path parallel to the road and look to the left for a definitive view of **Devil's Dyke**.

5 Head for the **South Downs Way** and turn left by a National Trust sign for **Summer Down** to a stile and gate. Follow the trail, keeping Devil's Dyke down to your left, and eventually you reach a stile leading into **Summer Down car park**.

Royal Oak

Nestling at the foot of the South Downs, close to the famous Devil's Dyke, this white-painted pub is popular in summer for its excellent barbecues. So, if walking this way on a fine summer Sunday, time your walk to coincide with the sizzling barbecue and relax with the family in the large garden, which has a huge marquee for a play area. The Royal Oak is a great community pub and you might happen upon their jazz lunches, charity bungee jumps and dancing Morris Men in the garden – it's that sort of place. The unpretentious and comfortably furnished bars are equally welcoming on less clement days, and you'll find Sussex-brewed Harveys Bitter on tap.

about the pub

Royal Oak
The Street, Poynings
Brighton, East Sussex BN45 7AQ
Tel: 01273 857389
www.royaloakpoynings.biz

DIRECTIONS: west of the village centre	
PARKING: 50	
OPEN: daily, all day	
FOOD: daily, all day Saturday and Sunday	
BREWERY/COMPANY: free house	
REAL ALE: Harveys Best, Greene King Abbot Ale and Old Speckled Hen	
DOGS: very welcome inside (biscuits offered)	

Food

Expect a varied menu that includes some good, hearty lunchtime snacks – thick-cut sandwiches, excellent cheese ploughman's (see the blackboard for the day's cheese selection), filled 'jackets', and 'best of British' meals – perhaps steak and kidney pie, beer-battered cod and local sausages and mash. Fresh dressed Selsey crab with crusty bread is a popular daily special.

Family facilities

Children are very welcome and the youngsters' menu is better than most, offering a child's portion of a roast on Sunday. There's a safe, large garden for summer days.

Alternative refreshment stops

The Devil's Dyke pub, three quarters of the way round the walk, has a family dining area and garden patio. Fish and chips, mixed grills and salads feature on the menu.

☛ Where to go from here

Explore the pair of windmills known as Jack and Jill at nearby Clayton. Jill Windmill is a restored post mill, originally constructed in Brighton in 1821 and moved to this location in 1852. She is still open for corn grinding demonstrations on summer Sundays, while her more solid, black-painted companion remains silent.

Ditchling Beacon and the Chattri War Memorial

One of the most spectacular sections of the South Downs, with views all the way.

Jack and Jill windmills

A hundred years ago the South Downs were dotted with windmills. These two are among the last to survive. Jill Windmill (www.jillwindmill.org.uk) is a wooden corn mill, restored to working order and open free of charge in the afternoon on most summer Sundays and bank holidays. Built in Brighton in 1821, it was originally called Lashmar's Mill. Neighbouring Jack Windmill is a brick tower mill, built in 1866 and now a private house, but you can see it from the car park. They both fell into disuse around 1906 and were probably first nicknamed Jack and Jill in the 1920s.

Chattri War Memorial

The white, Sicilian marble war memorial, inscribed in English and Hindi, is a strangely exotic feature in the Sussex countryside. Erected in 1921, it is dedicated to Indian servicemen who lost their lives in World War One. Some 4,000 were taken to a temporary hospital in Brighton's Royal Pavilion (which must have seemed a very strange place to find themselves in). The Hindus and Sikhs who did not survive were cremated here in funeral pyres sprinkled with symbolic, fruits, flowers and spices in accordance with their religious customs.

the ride

1 Turn left out of the car park, signposted **'public bridleway to Ditchling Beacon'**

and immediately ignore a private driveway on the left to Jack Windmill and another track to the left. Soon fork left uphill at a junction, signposted **South Downs Way** (the right turn goes to a farm). Blue arrow markers with acorn motifs denote the South Downs Way, which you follow for most of the ride. The track rises quite steeply at first and is stony, but it soon levels out and becomes less rough. There are huge views northwards over the Weald and you can see the Surrey hills in the distance. The escarpment is too steep for ploughing, and the wildlife is relatively undisturbed. Nine types of orchid, including the bee orchid (named for obvious reasons) grow hereabouts, and you may spot a pale blue chalkhill butterfly.

2 From **Ditchling Beacon car park** cross the road carefully and take the **South Downs Way** opposite. You will pass one of two dew ponds on the route: this is a man-made feature, created for livestock to drink from, and has a clay lining to stop water draining into the porous chalk. The route climbs up two grassy rises and drops slightly to cross a narrow farm road. From here it becomes clay rather than chalk on the surface, and can be sticky after rain.

3 After the next left, a descending fork (which you avoid), look for a **track** on the right, marked with a blue arrow which leads to a group of trees at the end of the field. This is the site of **Plumpton Plain**, a Bronze Age settlement. Carry on along the South Downs Way.

4 Just beyond a gate is a National Trust sign for **Black Cap**. Walk up to the summit by forking left to the **trig point**.

Enjoy the view which stretches to Seaford Head, a prominent, square-looking sea cliff, and to the Downs near Lewes. Return the same way, to **Ditchling Beacon**.

5 Unless you want to return along the South Downs Way, turn left at the very top of the main ascent after Ditchling Beacon (where **Jack Windmill** comes into view ahead). It's marked with a blue arrow and a sign for **'Chattri and the windmills'** just after another junction by a signpost on the right marked as the 'Keymer Post', while left is signposted to Brighton). Carry on down, with Brighton in view ahead, and at the second gate (with a waymarker symbol marked 'Chattri and the windmills' and with the number 13 on it), detour ahead to see the **Chattri war memorial**.

6 After the next gate, you'll see the memorial just down on your left. Leave your bike at the top and walk down. Return to the junction at the previous gate and turn left, following signs: the route bends right (number 44) on a fenced path slightly uphill, left (number 45), then downhill and turns right leaving the indicated route to 'Chattri and the windmills' (at number 46), which continues ahead. The track drops and rises, crossing the South Downs Way. passing through a farm to reach Jack and Jill windmills.

3h00 | 11 MILES | 17.7 KM | LEVEL 123

MAP: OS Explorer 122 South Downs Way: Steyning to Newhaven

START/FINISH: free car park by Jack and Jill windmills; grid ref: TQ 304134. Alternative start: Ditchling Beacon car park, south of Ditchling; grid ref: TQ 333131

TRAILS/TRACKS: quite bumpy chalk and grass tracks, with some sections along clay

LANDSCAPE: chalk downland

PUBLIC TOILETS: none on route

TOURIST INFORMATION: Brighton, tel: 0906 711 2255

CYCLE HIRE: Lifecycle, The Tile House, Preston Park, Preston Road, Brighton tel: 01273 542425 (www.lifecyclebrighton.com)

THE PUB: The Bull, Ditchling

❗ An energetic ride, with several ascents and descents – not suitable for young children

Getting to the start

Jack and Jill windmills: follow the A273 south from Hassocks, past junctions on the left with the B2112 and turning to Clayton, then turn left just before Pyecombe up Mill Lane. Ditchling Beacon: follow the B2112 south, then fork left on the road leading up to Ditchling Beacon. The car park is on the right at the very top (begin at Point **2**).

Why do this cycle ride?

This is a challenging ride, but don't be too put off by the beginning. After that there are some lovely sections on the grassy Downs on either side of Ditchling Beacon. You can either ride from Jack and Jill to Ditchling Beacon and back, continue to Black Cap, or go along tracks to the Chattri Indian war memorial and back to Jack and Jill.

Researched and written by: Tim Locke

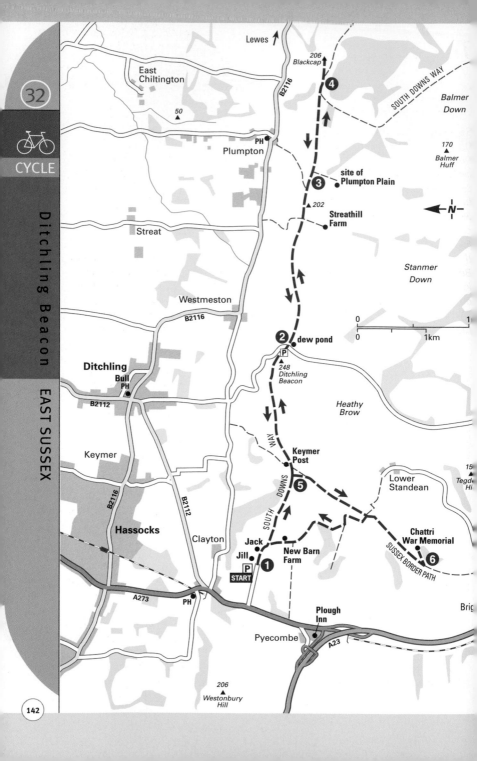

Lewes ↑

206
Blackcap
❹

SOUTH DOWNS WAY

Balmer Down

East Chiltington

50
▲

170
▲ *Balmer Huff*

PH
Plumpton

site of
Plumpton Plain
❸

—N→

▲ *202*

Streathill Farm

Streat

Stanmer Down

Westmeston

B2116

Ditchling

Bull
PH

B2112

0 ——————— 1
0 ——————— 1km

❷ dew pond
P
248 Ditchling Beacon

Heathy Brow

Keymer

SOUTH DOWNS WAY

Keymer Post
❺

Lower Standean

15
Tegde Hi

Chattri War Memorial
❻

SUSSEX BORDER PATH

Hassocks

B2112

Clayton

Jack

Jill
P
START
❶

New Barn Farm

A273

PH

Plough Inn

Bri

Pyecombe

A23

206
▲ *Westonbury Hill*

The Bull

Standing in a picturesque street in Ditchling, at the base of the South Downs, The Bull is a welcoming 14th-century beamed inn that has been comfortably refurbished. In the Inglenook Bar is an enormous fireplace with a roaring log fire in winter, low ceilings, old settles and dark wooden furnishings that give the room an ancient, time-worn feeling. Step into the Poacher's Bar and the décor is more modern, with large dining tables, Shaker-style chairs, an open fire and modern art lining the walls. Expect home-cooked food and four handpumped real ales.

about the pub

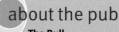

The Bull

2 High Street, Ditchling
Brighton, East Sussex BN6 8TZ
Tel: 01273 843147

DIRECTIONS: drive down to the A273, turn right towards Hassocks, then first right to Ditchling; the Bull is in the centre of the village, by the crossroads (park in the pub car park or the free public car park opposite). From Ditchling Beacon, turn left out of the car park and follow the road down to Ditchling

PARKING: 25

OPEN: daily; all day

FOOD: daily

BREWERY/COMPANY: free house

REAL ALE: Harveys Best, Greene King Old Speckled Hen, guest beers

ROOMS: 4 en suite

Food

The interesting menu includes sandwiches, dishes of marinated olives, home-made soups and main meals such as medallions of pork fillet with roasted vegetables, sausages and mash, and marinated halloumi, feta and vegetable brochette.

Family facilities

Children are welcome throughout the pub and smaller portions of adult dishes are available. Lovely sun-trap side terrace with views of the village and South Downs.

Alternative refreshment stops

There may be an ice-cream van in the car park at Ditchling Beacon.

☞ Where to go from here

Brighton (www.visitbrighton.com) is in view for much of this ride. It lies some 5 miles (8km) south and is an easy drive via the A23. In warmer months there's a lot happening along the waterfront, including beach volleyball, craft and books stalls and fortune tellers. The Royal Pavilion is a fantastically lavish seaside palace built by George IV, an Indian fantasy that becomes rather more Chinese inside. Just across the little park, there's the free Brighton Museum and Art Gallery which has something for everyone.

Hamsey and Barcombe Mills

Peaceful hamlets, mill pools, Roman sites, a pub that offers boat hire and a fair-weather extension to see a steam railway.

The Lavender Line

Old advertising signs and railway paraphernalia adorn the beautifully painted and restored station at Isfield. If you visit Cinders Buffet, on the platform, you can see 'before and after' photos that show how much volunteers and lovers of this little country railway have put into running a short section of the line that once ran from Lewes to Uckfield. Steam and diesel trains run during most weekends throughout the year, and on some other days during summer; one ticket allows you to ride all day. You can also go into the signal box at Isfield, try pulling the levers and operating a signal, while the former coal office houses a model railway layout. This ride crosses a bridge at Hamsey over the old railway (where the track has been removed), and from The Anchor Inn it follows a section along the trackbed itself (a licensed bridleway, which the landowner allows the public to use) to reach Barcombe Mills station, now a private house. You also cross twice over another line that ran from Lewes to East Grinstead.

Barcombe Mills

Two Roman roads – one from the west and the other from London – once met here. There was a mill here for 900 years until 1939; all that remains are the huge mill pool and gushing weirs. A plaque tells you this was, in 1066, the first place in Sussex

to have a tollgate: look out for the list of tolls by the bridge, showing charges in old money – 's' for a shilling (5p) and 'd' for a penny (12 pennies to the shilling).

the ride

1 With the Royal Oak pub on your right go along the main street in Barcombe and turn left in front of the village sign for **The Anchor Inn and Newick**. At the bottom of the hill turn right on Boast Lane, signposted Anchor Inn. After passing **Delves Farm**, and just before a house on the right, look for a track signposted '**bridleway**' on the left, into a triangular field. At the next triangular area, look to your left for a gate with a yellow arrow on it: at the far end of the field a line of hedgerow trees rising up to the top right skyline marks the line of a Roman road that ran from London to Lewes. Continue along the track, which later follows the left side of a field and passes a wartime **brick pillbox**. The route drops to a **footbridge**. Continue across a meadow to the gate ahead, up over another footbridge and along a track; ignore driveways to the right.

At the road T-junction turn right into **Isfield**. Pass the Laughing Fish pub on your left to visit the Lavender Line.

2 From Isfield retrace your route across the meadows and back past the pillbox. Turn left on the road to continue to **The Anchor Inn**.

3 Retrace your route a short distance from The Anchor Inn and, just before **Keeper's Cottage** on the left, turn left on the **old railway track**, signposted 'licensed bridleway to Barcombe Mills'.

4 On reaching a road opposite the old **Barcombe Mills station**, detour left and take the first road on the left. Turn right at the junction in front of the driveway to **Barcombe House** to reach the millpond and weirs of **Barcombe Mills**. Return the same way to the road, past **Barcombe Mills station**. At the next junction go straight ahead for a short-cut back into Barcombe. For the main route, turn left here, and pass

Isfield Station on the Lavender Line

CYCLE

Hamsey

EAST SUSSEX

3h00 · **12 MILES** · **19.3 KM** · **LEVEL 2**

SHORTER ALTERNATIVE ROUTE

1h00 · **4 MILES** · **6.4 KM** · **LEVEL 2**

MAP: OS Explorer 122 South Downs Way: Steyning to Newhaven

START/FINISH: Barcombe village centre; roadside parking; grid ref: TQ 418157

TRAILS/TRACKS: back lanes, hard stony track; optional extension along a track and through fields that get muddy after rain

LANDSCAPE: farmland and river, with distant views of the South Downs

PUBLIC TOILETS: none; when open, Barcombe Mills station has toilets

TOURIST INFORMATION: Lewes tel: 01273 483448

CYCLE HIRE: Lifecycle, The Tile House, Preston Park, Preston Road, Brighton tel: 01273 542425 (www.lifecyclebrighton.com)

THE PUB: The Anchor Inn, Barcombe

🕕 One short climb after Barcombe Mills, otherwise more gentle ups and downs. Take care on blind bends

Getting to the start

Barcombe is signposted from the A26 and A275, 4.3 miles (7km) north of Lewes.

Why do this cycle ride?

Along this route of quiet lanes you'll find everything from Roman sites to wartime defences. Off-road sections follow a disused track, with distant views of the South Downs, and an ancient 'green lane' that crosses fields and leads to the Lavender Line preserved railway.

Researched and written by: Tim Locke

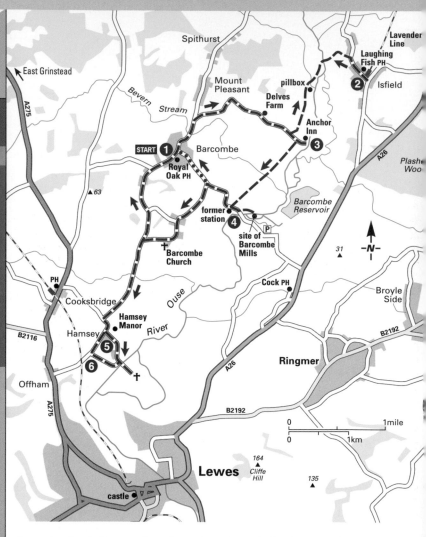

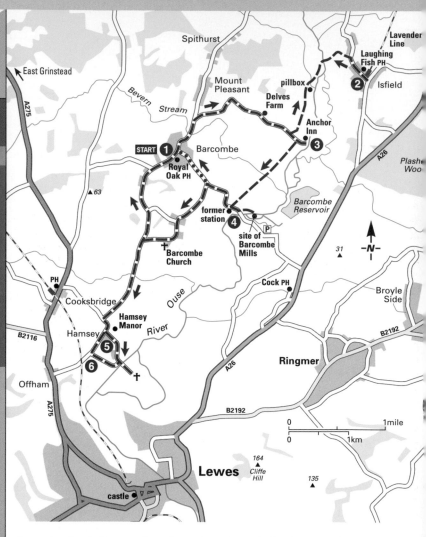

Barcombe church. Carry on along the road, keeping left at the next two junctions towards Hamsey.

5 Just after **Hamsey Manor** turn left down Whitfeld Lane to Hamsey. There is a lovely half-timbered house called **Yeoman's** dated 1584; just after, turn left at a T-junction. The road crosses a former canal via a bridge. After the bridge, you can pick up the keys to **Hamsey church** from **Pine Barn,** the first house on the left. The road rises over the old railway to reach Hamsey church, a wonderful example of what medieval country churches used to look like. Return to **Hamsey,** keep left at the road junction by the **canal bridge,** past a pillbox.

6 Turn right at the T-junction, and after **Whitfeld Lane** joins from the right follow signs for Barcombe to return to the start.

CYCLE

33

Hamsey   EAST SUSSEX

146

The Anchor Inn

The white-painted Anchor, built in 1790 mainly to cater for the bargees, has an idyllic location in an isolated spot on the west bank of the River Ouse. It lost its liquor licence in 1895, after the landlord was convicted of smuggling, and didn't regain it until 1963. Refurbished after serious flooding in 2000, the interior features wood and flagstone floors, a warm décor, open fires and a welcoming atmosphere. The big attraction here is the large riverside decking area with views directly to the river and the open countryside beyond, The pub also has 27 boats available for hire by the hour.

Food

Expect classic pub food such as baked trout, cottage pie, chilli, lasagne and various steaks. There are also good snacks and daily specials.

Family facilities

The Anchor Inn has a children's licence so youngsters are welcome anywhere in the pub. There is a basic children's menu and smaller portions of adult dishes are offered. The large front garden is ideal for children; take care by the river.

about the pub

The Anchor Inn
Anchor Lane, Barcombe
Lewes, East Sussex BN8 5BS
Tel: 01273 400414
www.anchorinnandboating.co.uk

DIRECTIONS: The Anchor Inn is at the end of Boast Lane (which becomes Anchor Lane), all by itself, and signposted from the centre of Barcombe village

PARKING: 100

OPEN: daily; all day Easter to September; all day Saturday and Sunday only October to Easter. Phone for winter weekday opening times

FOOD: no food Sunday evening

BREWERY/COMPANY: free house

REAL ALE: Harveys Best, Badger Tanglefoot

ROOMS: 3 rooms (1 en suite)

Alternative refreshment stops

The Royal Oak in Barcombe and the Laughing Fish in Isfield both serve pub food and have gardens. Cinders Buffet at Isfield Station has good-value snacks and light lunches.

☛ Where to go from here

About 4.3 miles (7km) south of Barcombe, Lewes Castle (www.sussexpast.co.uk) stands at the high point of the hilly, ancient town of Lewes. Your entrance ticket includes Barbican House Museum, with its scale model of 19th-century Lewes. The town of Lewes itself is fun to explore, with its many tiny lanes and paths.

From Firle Place to Charleston Farmhouse

Climb high above a sprawling estate and look towards distant horizons on this superb downland walk.

Feudal Firle and decorated Charleston

Stroll along the South Downs Way between Alfriston and the River Ouse and you can look down towards the sleepy village of Firle, nestling amid a patchwork of fields and hedgerows below the escarpment. There is something that sets this place apart from most other communities. Firle is an estate village with a tangible feudal atmosphere.

At the centre of the village is Firle Place, home to the Gage family for over 500 years and now open to the public. The 18th-century house is magnificent, though it hardly looks classically English. It's built of a pale stone specially imported from Caen in Normandy, with hipped roof, dormers and a splendid Venetian window surmounting the rusticated central archway in the east front. Firle Place is surrounded by glorious parkland and set against a magnificent backdrop of hanging woods. No house could occupy a finer location. A tour of the house reveals some fascinating treasures. The paintings include a collection of old masters with works by Van Dyck, Gainsborough, Reynolds and Rubens and there are also collections of Sèvres porcelain and English and French furniture.

Charleston Farmhouse is also open to the public, and provides a complete contrast to Firle. It was the rustic home in the early 20th century to artists Duncan Grant and Clive and Vanessa Bell, members of the Bloomsbury Set. They personalised the house by painting murals and decorating the furniture.

Above: 18th-century Firle Place

he walk

1 Turn left out of the car park, pass **The Ram Inn** and follow the road round to the right, rough the village of **Firle**. Pass the village ores, a footpath to Charleston, and a path Firle's **Church of St Peter**, all on the left, nd continue heading southwards out of e village.

2 Turn right at a junction of concrete tracks and make for the road. Turn left, ead for the downland escarpment and egin the long climb, steep in places. On aching the car park at the top, swing left a **gate** and join the **South Downs Way**.

3 Head eastwards on the long distance trail and to **Firle Beacon**, passing a **trig oint**. Look out for a bridleway crossing ver the South Downs Way and bear left.

what to look for

In Firle's main street is the quaint old village stores. Until the time when cars began to make shopping in towns and cities easier, Firle benefitted from a tailor, a bootmaker, a butcher and a baker. A blacksmith, a miller and a harness maker also operated in the village.

It's always pleasing to find a church open to visitors, and the sign at the entrance to Firle's church states that the door is open from dawn to dusk. The parish refuses 'to be deterred by occasional thefts, believing it must be available to the people of the village.' The church includes a window dedicated to Henry Rainald Gage KCVO, the 6th Viscount who succeeded to the title in his 17th year in 1912 and died in 1982. The window was designed by John Piper and is possibly his last work in stained glass.

3h30 — **6.5 MILES** — **10.4 KM** — **LEVEL 123 3**

WALK

MAP: OS Explorer 123 South Down Ways: Newhaven to Eastbourne

START/FINISH: free car park, Firle; grid ref: TQ 468075

PATHS: tracks, paths and roads

LANDSCAPE: downland and farmland

PUBLIC TOILETS: Firle Place and Charleston Farmhouse

TOURIST INFORMATION: Lewes tel: 01273 483448

THE PUB: The Ram Inn, Firle

🛈 Long, occasionally steep ascent and descent of the South Downs escarpment. Best tackled by older family groups as the walk is quite long

Getting to the start

West Firle is signposted south off the A27 between Lewes and Eastbourne, 5 miles (8km) east of Lewes. Pass the entrance to Firle Place on the left, bearing slightly right. The entrance to the village car park is about 50yds (46m) further on, on the left.

Researched and written by:
Nick Channer, David Halford

West Firle

EAST SUSSEX

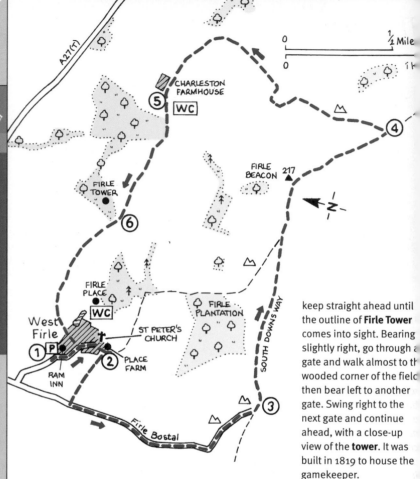

keep straight ahead until the outline of **Firle Tower** comes into sight. Bearing slightly right, go through a gate and walk almost to the wooded corner of the field, then bear left to another gate. Swing right to the next gate and continue ahead, with a close-up view of the **tower**. It was built in 1819 to house the gamekeeper.

4 Make for a gate and head diagonally down the escarpment. Aim for a gate and skirt a belt of **woodland** before continuing straight on at a junction of tracks. Pass a house called **Tilton Meadow** and bear left at the next junction, after a large hay barn. Follow the concrete bridleway to a right-angled bend, then swing immediately left towards **Charleston Farmhouse**, once home to members of the Bloomsbury Set.

5 Pass a car park on the right, climb over a gate with **farm barns** on the left, and

6 Make for a line of trees and briefly pick your way between them to the edge of a field. Keep to the right-hand edge of the field and make for a gap by some **houses**. Go through a wrought-iron gate by the side of a **brick and flint cottage** and cross the lane to a footpath and gate. Follow the waymarked path across the parkland, cross the main drive and follow the sign for the **church**. Look for a kissing gate and track and follow it to the road. Turn right and return to the car park at Firle

The Ram Inn

Built of brick and flint and partly tile-hung, The Ram displays a fascinating mixture of periods. The Georgian part was once the local courthouse. Other parts are older – the kitchen dates back nearly 500 years – and there are 14 staircases in this rambling former coach stop. The main bar is a simple, unpretentious affair with a motley collection of tables and chairs and old photos, huge log fires and a comfortably worn and very relaxed atmosphere. Expect few modern-day intrusions here, but all the time-honoured amusements – traditional darts, dominoes, shove halfpenny and toad-in-the-hole. It's not smart, but the Harveys beer is tip-top, the welcome to booted walkers and families is genuinely warm and friendly. A charming flint-walled garden with rustic tables makes an idyllic spot for summer drinking.

Food

Menu choices range through burgers, pasta and varieties of ploughman's to fish and chips, turkey and ham pie, and beef stew and dumplings. Afternoon cream teas.

Family facilities

Children are truly spoilt here – there are toddler, child and hungry small adult menus, and a huge play/family room with microwave and toys. The safe rear garden has play equipment, and the added attractions of a tame goose and cat.

Alternative refreshment stops

Firle Place has a licensed restaurant serving lunches and cream teas. There's also a tea room at Charleston Farmhouse.

☞ Where to go from here

The attractive medieval town of Lewes has many quaint corners to explore, a splendid castle dating back to Norman times, and an intriguing museum in a lovely timber-framed house that once belonged to Anne of Cleves (www.sussexpast.co.uk).

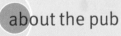

about the pub

The Ram Inn
Firle, Lewes
East Sussex BN8 6NS
Tel: 01273 858222

DIRECTIONS: on the road into the village, near the car park at the start of the walk

PARKING: use village car park

OPEN: daily, all day

FOOD: daily, all day Friday, Saturday and Sunday

BREWERY/COMPANY: free house

REAL ALE: Harveys Sussex

DOGS: welcome inside on a lead

Cuckmere Haven and the Seven Sisters Country Park

WALK

Cuckmere Haven

EAST SUSSEX

Follow a breezy trail beside the Cuckmere River.

Cuckmere Haven

Cuckmere Haven is one of the few undeveloped river mouths in the south east. It was used by smugglers in the 18th century to bring ashore brandy and lace. The scene has changed little, with the eternal surge of waves breaking on the isolated shore. Cuckmere River joins the English Channel here but not before it makes a series of extraordinarily wide loops through water-meadows – earning it the occasional epithet 'Snake River'. Winding ever closer to the sea, the Cuckmere emerges beside the white chalk cliffs known as the Seven Sisters. There are, in fact, eight of these, with the highest, Haven Brow (253ft/77m), closest to the river mouth. On the other side of the estuary rise Seaford Head cliffs, now a nature reserve.

The focal point of the lower valley is Seven Sisters Country Park, 692 acres (280ha) imaginatively planned to blend with the coastal beauty of this area. There are artificial lakes and park trails, and a visitor centre with many interesting exhibits and displays. Wildlife plays a key role, providing naturalists with many hours of enjoyment. The flowers and insects here are at their best in early to mid-summer, while spring and autumn are a good time for views of migrant birds.

Early migrant wheatears may be spotted in the vicinity of the river mouth from late February onwards, and are followed later by martins, swallows, whinchats and warblers. Keep a careful eye out for whitethroats, terns and waders, too. The lakes and lagoons tend to attract waders such as curlews, sandpipers and little stints. Grey phalaropes have also been seen in the park, usually after severe autumn storms. These elusive birds spend most of their lives far out to sea, usually off South America or western Africa.

The walk explores this part of the Cuckmere Valley and begins by heading for the beach. As you make your way there, you might wonder why the river meanders the way it does. The meltwaters of the last Ice Age shaped the landscape and over the centuries rising sea levels and a freshwater peat swamp influenced the river's route to the Channel. Around the start of the 19th century the sea rose to today's level, and a new straight cut with raised banks shortened the Cuckmere's journey. This unnatural waterway controls the river and helps prevent flooding in the valley.

the walk

1 Make for the gate near the entrance to the **Seven Sisters Country Park** and follow the wide, grassy path towards the beach. The path gradually curves to the right, running alongside a **concrete track**. The Cuckmere River meanders beside you, heading for the open sea. Continue ahead

1h30 — **3 MILES** — **4.8 KM** — **LEVEL 1**23

MAP: OS Explorer 123 South Downs Way: Newhaven to Eastbourne

START/FINISH: fee-paying car park opposite the Seven Sisters Country Park visitor centre, at Exceat; grid ref: TV 518995

PATHS: grassy trails and well-used paths; mostly beside the Cuckmere or canalised branch of river

LANDSCAPE: exposed and isolated valley and river mouth

PUBLIC TOILETS: opposite car park, by visitor centre

TOURIST INFORMATION: Seaford, tel: 01323 897426

THE PUB: Golden Galleon, Exceat Bridge

🛑 Suitable for children of all ages

Getting to the start

The visitor centre for the Seven Sisters Country Park is just east of the turning at Exceat on the A259 which is signed to Westdean and Alfriston. Park on the south side of the A259, by the green phone-box.

Researched and written by:
Nick Channer, David Halford

what to look for

Shingle plants thrive on the sheltered parts of beaches, and a stroll at Cuckmere Haven reveals the yellow horned-poppy and the fleshy leaved sea kale. Sea beet, curled dock and scentless camomile also grow here. If you have the time, take a look at the Seaford Head Nature Reserve, which lies on the west side of Cuckmere Haven. This chalk headland, which rises 282ft (85m) above the sea, is a popular local attraction and from here the coastal views are magnificent.

Left: Cuckmere Haven where smugglers operated during the 18th century

between the track and the river and make for a **South Downs Way sign**.

2 Avoid the long distance trail as it runs in from the left, pass it and the **Foxhole campsite** and keep ahead, through the gate towards the beach. Veer left at the **beach** and South Downs Way sign. On reaching the next gate, don't go through it. Instead, keep right and follow the beach sign. Pass a couple of **wartime pill-boxes** on the left, an evocative reminder of less peaceful times, and go through a gate. Join a stony path and walk ahead to the beach, with the white cliff walls of the **Seven Sisters** rearing up beside you.

3 Turn right and cross the shore, approaching a **Cuckmere Haven**

Emergency Point sign. Branch off to the right to join another track here. Follow this for about 50yds (46m) until you come to a junction and keep left, following the **Habitat Trail** and **Park Trail** (not signed). Keep beside the **Cuckmere** – the landscape here is characterised by a network of meandering channels and waterways, all feeding into the river. Pass a turning for Foxhole campsite and follow the footpath as it veers left, in line with the Cuckmere. Make for a kissing gate and continue on the straight path by the side of the river.

4 Keep ahead to the road at **Exceat Bridge** and on the left is the **Golden Galleon** pub. Turn right and follow the A259 to return to the car park at the country park

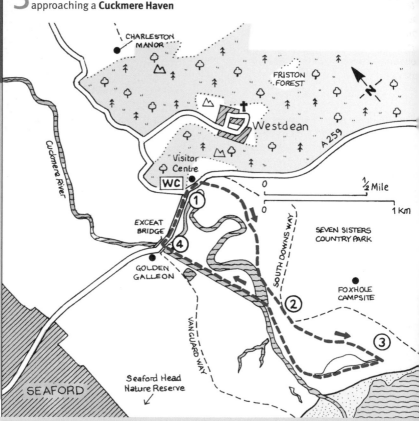

Golden Galleon

is 18th-century inn is a popular
freshment stop for walkers tackling
e South Downs Way, and enjoys
agnificent views down the Cuckmere
tuary to the sea. Formerly a shepherd's
othy, it has grown enough to comfortably
ccommodate TV crews making an
isode of Eastenders, a Gary Rhodes
ommercial and a Dickens costume
rama. The pub is also thought to have
spired Rudyard Kipling's poem 'Song
the Smugglers'. High-trussed and
tched rafters create an airy feel to the
acious and smartly modernised main
ar. But the place to be after this walk is
t in the sloping garden, soaking up the
ews and refreshing pints of Harveys
ussex Bitter.

about the pub

Golden Galleon
Exceat Bridge, Seaford
East Sussex BN25 4AB
Tel: 01323 892247
www.mbplc.com

DIRECTIONS: immediately west of Exceat
Bridge on the A259

PARKING: 100

OPEN: daily, all day

FOOD: daily, all day

BREWERY/COMPANY: Mitchells & Butler

REAL ALE: Bass, Harveys Sussex, Adnams
Bitter

DOGS: allowed in a designated area in the
pub and the garden

Food

Printed menus list a broad range of
traditional pub food. Typically, choose
from an imaginative range of sandwiches
(chicken, mozzarella, tomato and pesto –
served until 5pm), 'small plates' like soups,
salads and fishcakes, and 'large plates',
such as sausages and mash, beef,
mushroom and ale pie, and sirloin
steak with peppercorn sauce.

Family facilities

Children are welcome in the pub, and
families will find a range of children's
dishes chalked up on a blackboard, and
baby-changing facilities in the toilets.

Alternative refreshment stops

The visitor centre at the Seven Sisters
Country Park has a restaurant and
tea rooms.

☛ Where to go from here

Paradise Park and Gardens at Newhaven
(www.paradisepark.co.uk) has gardens to
explore, plus interactive displays and
dinosaurs which move at Planet Earth, and
rides and amusements for youngsters.

The Cuckoo Trail around Hailsham

CYCLE

Well-signposted tracks and lanes link together to create a cycle-friendly ride along a railway track and through peaceful countryside to Michelham Priory.

The Cuckoo Trail

Part of the National Cycle Network, this well-signposted and popular route follows a former railway for most of its 11 miles (17.7km) between Heathfield and Polegate, with an extension to Eastbourne. The railway opened in 1880, linking Polegate with Eridge, and got its name because of a Sussex tradition that says the first cuckoo of spring was always heard at Heathfield Fair. The line closed in 1968, but was revived imaginatively in 1990 as a cycle path, shared with walkers. Quirky iron sculptures and carved wooden benches punctuate the route. Signposted by a former station, the Old Loom Mill complex has a café, crafts, playground, bike hire a the MasterPiece Studio where you can pa your own pottery and collect the results after firing a day or so later.

Michelham Priory

Despite its name, this is a Tudor mansion set in England's longest medieval, water-filled moat and approached through a 14th-century gatehouse. Wander around the grounds and you will find a physic herb garden with plants that were used fo medicine and cooking, re-created Iron Ag huts, and the remains of the original prior where Augustinian canons once lived and worshipped. Inside the house are tapestrie kitchen equipment and an 18th-century child's bedroom; by the entrance is a working watermill which grinds flour for sa

the ride

1 From the car park, return along the ma **driveway** to the road. Turn left and kee left at the first junction. Just after the next junction, turn left on to **Robin Post Lane**, and follow the **'cycle route 2'** signs. The surfacing ends after **New House Farm** on the right. Continue on a track, turning righ at the next junction signposted **Cuckoo Trail/route 2**; you can see the South Down away to the right in the distance.

The Cuckoo Trail has several unique sculptures along its route

Michelham Priory is actually a Tudor mansion with the remains of the original priory

2 At the end of the forest, where there is a house away to the right, ignore a track to the left but keep forward on **cycle route 2**. Beneath the embankment of the A22 turn right on a cycle path, following **Cuckoo Trail signs** which lead you under the main road and along the right side of a road. Avoid crossing a footbridge over the **A27** Polegate bypass and continue on the cycle path. At the next bridge turn left on the **Cuckoo Trail** and follow for 3 miles (4.8km) to Hailsham. The Cuckoo Trail itself is very well signposted and easy to follow. It follows the old railway track for much of the way, but occasionally diverts along small and quiet residential roads. Cross over via **traffic lights**. Later the Trail leaves the old railway track briefly and you enter **Freshfield Close**; follow the Cuckoo Trail signs to right and then to the left.

3 The Trail follows a road close to a **duck pond** and the small park surrounding it, then just after the Railway Tavern on the right, it turns left to leave the road, passing close to a **skateboard ramp**. Going under a bridge, it continues along the old railway track. After some playing fields appear on the right, the Cuckoo Trail bends left into a **housing estate**, then right and left on a **path**.

4 Go under **Hawk's Road bridge** and turn left up the ramp, signposted **Michelham Priory**. Turn right on the road, then forward at the mini-roundabout to follow **Hempstead Lane**.

3h15 — **11 MILES** — **17.7 KM** — **LEVEL 2**

SHORTER ALTERNATIVE ROUTE

3h00 — **9.5 MILES** — **15.3 KM** — **LEVEL 2**

MAP: OS Explorer 122, South Downs Way: Newhaven to Eastbourne

START/FINISH: Abbot's Wood car park; grid ref: TQ 558072

TRAILS/TRACKS: largely compacted gravel and earth tracks, muddy in places; some quiet back lanes and residential roads

LANDSCAPE: woodland, farmland, railway track, suburban roads

PUBLIC TOILETS: at the start

TOURIST INFORMATION: Eastbourne, tel: 01323 411400

CYCLE HIRE: MP Cycle Hire (passed on the Cuckoo Trail), the MasterPiece Studio, Old Loom Mill, Ersham Road, Hailsham BN27 4RG, tel: 01323 449245 or 07974 443119

THE PUB: The Old Oak Inn, Arlington

🛈 Often muddy for a short section after Point 5. Use the bike crossing point on the A22 at the edge of Hailsham, and take special care as this road is usually busy

Getting to the start

Abbot's Wood car park is signposted from the A27 between Lewes and Polegate. Take the north turn (Thornwell Road), signposted Arlington and Abbot's Wood. Keep left at the first road junction and right at the next junction, then soon turn right at the signpost to Abbot's Wood car park.

Why do this cycle ride?

The ride uses the Cuckoo Trail and is easy to cycle as most of it is on a disused railway track.

Researched and written by: Tim Locke

Hailsham   EAST SUSSEX

5 At the **A22** dual carriageway, cross very carefully by the traffic islands indicated with blue bicycle/pedestrian symbols, and take the lane signposted to **Michelham Priory** opposite. The road surfacing ends by the last cottage on the left, and the lane continues as an often muddy track. Just after the track bears left, ignore a bridleway forking right, and continue along to a road. Before turning right along the road, you can detour left for a short distance to see the entrance to **Arlington Stadium**, a venue for stock-car racing and speedway.

6 At the next junction detour right to **Michelham Priory**, then right again at the access road to the Priory itself. Return to the previous road junction and turn right towards Arlington and Wilmington, past **The Old Oak Inn**. Take the next left to return to Abbot's Wood car park.

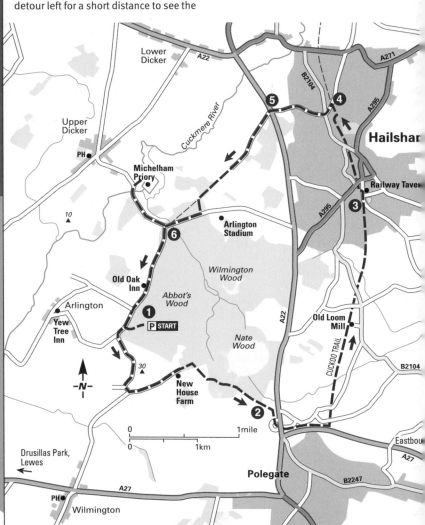

The Old Oak Inn

Built in 1733 as the village almshouse, the Old Oak became a pub in the early 1900s and supplied ale and cider to the workers in the local brick-making and charcoal-burning industries. The friendly, open-plan bar has big beams, blazing winter log fires, comfortable seating and a relaxed atmosphere. Ales are tapped from the cask and you will find a good choice of time-honoured pub games to while away an hour or two on inclement days. In sunny weather head out into the secluded rear garden and savour the South Downs views.

about the pub

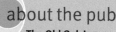

The Old Oak Inn
Arlington, Polegate
East Sussex BN26 6SJ
Tel: 01323 482072

DIRECTIONS: follow directions to Abbots Wood car park (above), go past Abbots Wood for 0.5 mile (0.8km) and it's on the left side of the road

PARKING: 40

OPEN: daily; all day

FOOD: daily; all day Saturday and Sunday

BREWERY/COMPANY: free house

REAL ALE: Harveys Best, Badger Best, guest beers

Food

The menu offers light meals such as ploughman's salads and filled baguettes. More substantial dishes include 'Oak Favourites' like ham, egg and chips, home-made fishcakes and a large Yorkshire pudding filled with Cumberland sausage and rich gravy. Alternatives range from the daily curry and mixed grill to blackboard specials like seafood gratin and lamb shank in minted gravy.

Family facilities

Children of all ages are welcome inside. There are high chairs, children's portions of main menu dishes, a menu for young children and a wooden adventure frame and slide in the garden.

Alternative refreshment stops

The Railway Arms in Hailsham has a children's area in the garden, and there's a café with a playground at Old Loom Mill on the Cuckoo Trail and a café for visitors at Michelham Priory.

☛ Where to go from here

Four miles (6.4km) south west of Abbot's Wood, Drusillas Park (www.drusillas.co.uk), on the road to Alfriston, has a wonderful animal collection. Animals are kept in conditions similar to those they would experience in the wild. There are monkeys, meerkats, a farmyard area, and 'Penguin Bay' with underwater viewing points, plus play areas, a miniature railway and a paddling pool.

Friston Forest and Cuckmere Haven

Three wonderful contrasts: the Cuckmere river, as it meanders its way to the sea, the tranquil greenery of Friston Forest, and the sweeping views from the top of the South Downs.

Cuckmere Haven

The winding Cuckmere River ends at Cuckmere Haven, the only undeveloped estuary in Sussex, where there is a glorious view along the bottom of the Seven Sisters to the left and the cottages on Seaford Head to the right. The beach is shingle and shelves quite steeply, so this is for stronger swimmers only. During the war, a mock town with lights was built here to mislead enemy bombers into raiding this instead of Newhaven; there are still fortifications here, including concrete 'dragon teeth' tank traps seen to the right, just before the beach. The meadows, reed beds and ponds are important habitats for wildlife. As you approach the beach you will pass an artificial lagoon, made in 1975, and a nesting and feeding area for birds.

Friston Forest and Westdean village

The forest was planted in the early 20th century over an underground reservoir: at some points on the route you can see the waterworks and water tower. Westdean is a secluded village surrounded by the forest. Next to the church stands a rectory dating

Above: A family day out along safe paths

from the late 13th century.

the ride

1 From the car park go down towards the vehicular entrance, and just before the road turn right on a track signposted '**public bridleway to Westdean**'. Look out for the bicycle symbols in green, which denote the bike trail you will be following for the first part of the ride.

2 At the first house at Westdean keep forward on the track (signposted **Excea Hill**), following the green bike symbols. After 1 mile (1.6km) reach a junction marked with five tall red-and-white posts.

3 For a short return to **Westdean**, fork left almost immediately after, and continue following the **green bike symbols**, turning right at the hard forest road (to the left you can see the tall **red and white posts**), then soon left at another bike symbol. The track rises (at the top a short path leads up right to a **viewpoint** over the forest and to the sea) and then falls. Leave the waymarked trail at a three-way fork, keeping right downhill, past a barrier and houses, then turn right at a road junction into Westdean. Pass the **church** and rectory and drop to a T-junction by **Pond Cottage**, then go ahead towards the flight of steps, where you turn right along the track you were following earlier and retrace to the start.

For the main route, continue ahead at Point 3 and fork left near some **power lines**. Go past a barrier, and forward again on joining a metalled road, which becomes less surfaced (ignore side turns). On reaching a road, turn left along it to **Jevington**. Note the blue plaque on the

4h00	12 MILES	19.3 KM	LEVEL 1 2 3

SHORTER ALTERNATIVE ROUTE

2h00	7 MILES	11.3 KM	LEVEL 1 2 3

MAP: OS Explorer 123, South Downs Way: Newhaven to Eastbourne

START/FINISH: Seven Sisters Country Park pay car park (on north side of A259; grid ref: TV 518995

TRAILS/TRACKS: well drained, compacted earth and forest tracks, level concrete track to Cuckmere Haven; short downhill road section, steep rough tracks and two stony descents on the long ride

LANDSCAPE: forest, riverside, shingle beach, open chalk downland

PUBLIC TOILETS: at the start

TOURIST INFORMATION: Eastbourne, tel: 01323 411400

CYCLE HIRE: The Cuckmere Cycle Company (by Visitor Centre), tel: 01323 870310; www.cuckmere-cycle.co.uk

THE PUB: The Plough and Harrow, Litlington

⚠ Cycle carefully and give pedestrians on the track to Cuckmere Haven priority at busy times. The full ride on the South Downs Way is unsuitable for younger children

Getting to the start

From the A259 between Eastbourne and Seaford, turn off at Seven Sisters Country Park, behind the visitor centre, and immediately turn right for the car park.

Why do this cycle ride?

On this route you will find deep, varied forest laced with cycle paths, and a level, easy ride to the shingle beach at Cuckmere Haven for a famous view of the Seven Sisters.

Researched and written by: Tim Locke

Hungry Monk restaurant, informing you this was the birthplace of banoffee pie in 1972.

4 Turn left at Jevington and take the track signposted **South Downs Way** and church: inside there is a 1,000-year-old stone carving of Christ stabbing a beast AD 950), the triumph of Good over Evil. Continue uphill on the South Downs Way, which steepens through the woods (too steep for cycling). Ignore side turns.

5 At the top, emerge from the **woodland**, ignore the South Downs Way to the right and keep forward. There are wonderful views inland and towards the sea from this track, and just to the left is **Lullington Heath Nature Reserve,** where there is an unusual combination of plants because of the acidic conditions on the chalky soil. The track later drops steeply and then rises up to a junction by a small **flint pillar** on the left. Slightly hidden to the right is **Winchester's Pond**, a small pond that is the haunt of dragonflies. Carry on ahead and downhill, forking left

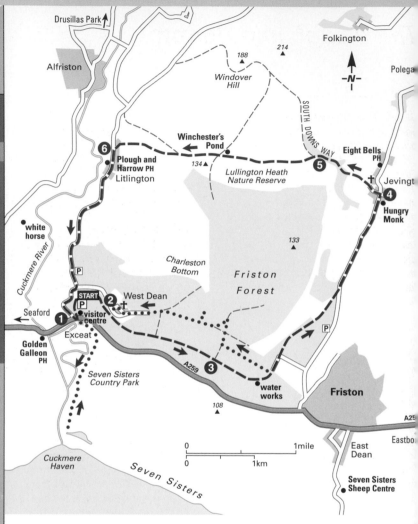

later to **Litlington**, where the track twists left and then right by **farm buildings**.

6 At the road, turn left through Litlington, past the tea gardens and **The Plough and Harrow** pub. As you continue along the road you can see the figure of a **white horse** etched into the hillside across the valley. The road leads back to the turning to Westdean and the car park at Exceat. To

extend the ride, wheel your bike between the restaurant and **visitor centre** on a brick path to the main road. Cross very carefully and take the gate opposite, near the bus stop. The concrete track leads towards the **sea**. Keep right at two forks, following a bicycle route to the **beach**. Return the same way.

The Plough and Harrow

Gloriously situated on the edge of the South Downs, this extended 15th-century brick-and-flint pub stands in sleepy Litlington in a secluded spot in the Cuckmere Valley. Original wattle-and-daub walls and a large open fireplace in the small original building hint at the pub's old age, while the carpeted, low beamed lounge and 'railway dining-car' restaurant in the more modern extension are tastefully furnished. There is a suntrap front garden and an attractive rear lawn with smart benches and umbrellas for summer drinking.

about the pub

The Plough and Harrow
Litlington, Alfriston
East Sussex BN26 5RE
Tel: 01323 870632

DIRECTIONS: the pub is on the full ride; if you are following the short ride, load up your bikes and turn right out of the car park to get there, or cycle there (an easy 1.6 miles/2.5km each way). It is on the left of the road, near the church

PARKING: 50

OPEN: daily; all day Saturday and Sunday

FOOD: daily

BREWERY/COMPANY: free house

REAL ALE: Harveys Bitter, Badger Tanglefoot, Greene King Old Speckled Hen, guest beer

Food
Good, wholesome pub fare includes ploughman's lunches, home-made pies (steak and Harveys stout), fresh battered cod, dressed Cromer crab with chilli and lemon oil, and Sussex smokies – smoked haddock, cream and potatoes with cheese topping.

Family facilities
Children are very welcome inside and there's a children's menu available.

Alternative refreshment stops
Exceat Farmhouse Restaurant (by the visitor centre) serves meals and snacks. You can also try Litlington Tea Garden in Litlington, the Eight Bells, Jevington, just off route, or the Golden Galleon at Exceat, just west of the start, via the A259 (see page 155).

☞ Where to go from here
South east from Exceat is the Seven Sisters Sheep Centre (www.sheepcentre.co.uk), one of the world's largest collections of sheep, with many rare breeds and other farm animals. Visit the Clergy House in Alfriston (www.nationaltrust.org.uk), or visit Drusillas Park (www.drusillas.co.uk), one of the best small zoos in the country.

A circuit from Wilmington

This downland walk visits a legendary chalk figure which has baffled archaeologists and historians for hundreds of years.

The Long Man of Wilmington

One of Britain's most impressive and enduring mysteries is the focal point of this glorious walk high on the Downs. Cut into the turf below Windover Hill, the chalk figure of the Long Man of Wilmington is the largest representation of the human figure in western Europe and yet it remains an enigma, its origins shrouded in mystery. For centuries experts have been trying to solve this ancient puzzle but no one has been able to prove who he is or what he symbolises.

The earliest drawing, made in 1710 by John Rowley, a surveyor, suggests that the original figure was a shadow or indentation in the grass rather than a bold line. It seems there were distinguishing facial features which may have long faded; the staves being held were not a rake and a scythe as once described and the head was originally a helmet shape, indicating that the Long Man may have been a helmeted war-god. Until the 19th century the figure was only visible in a certain light, particularly when there was a dusting of snow or frost on the ground. The Long Man's ghostly aura, the chill, wintry conditions and the remoteness of these surroundings would surely have been enough to send a shiver down the spine. In 1874, a public subscription was raised through *The Times* and the figure re-cut. To help define the outline of the Long Man, the site was marked out in yellow bricks, though this restoration work may have incorrectly positioned the feet. In 1969 further restoration work began and the yellow bricks were replaced with pre-cast concrete blocks. These are frequently painted now, so that the shape of the Long Man stands out from a considerable distance away.

Photographed from the air, the figure is elongated, but when viewed from ground level, by an optical illusion he assumes normal human proportions. The walk passes as close as it can to the Long Man before heading out into isolated downland country.

the walk

1 Make for the car park exit and follow the path parallel to the road, heading towards the **Long Man**. Bear left at the next gate and take the Wealdway to the chalk figure. Climb quite steeply, curving to the right. Go through a gate, avoid the Wealdway arrow and go straight ahead towards the escarpment, veering right just below the Long Man.

Below: The Long Man at Wilmington, of unknown age, was renovated with white bricks in 1874

3h00 · **6.25 MILES** · **10.1 KM** · **LEVEL 1 2 3**

2 Go through the next gate, cross a **track** and bear left on reaching a fence. A few paces brings you to a gate and a sign for the **South Downs Way**. Pass a small reservoir and follow the track to the road.

3 Turn left and walk down to a signpost for **Lullington church**, following the path beside several cottages. After visiting the church, retrace your steps to the road and turn right. Head down the lane and look for **Alfriston church** on the right. Pass a turning to the village on the right and continue ahead towards Seaford. Look out for a **postbox** and swing left here, signposted '**Jevington**'.

4 Follow the **bridleway** as it climbs steadily between tracts of remote downland. Keep left at the next main junction and there is a moderate climb. Avoid the bridle track branching off to the left and continue ahead towards Jevington. **Lullington Heath National Nature Reserve** is on the right now. Pass a bridleway to **Charleston Bottom** on the right and keep

MAP: OS Explorer 123 South Downs Way: Newhaven to Eastbourne

START/FINISH: long-stay car park, Wilmington; grid ref: TQ 543041

PATHS: downland paths and tracks, stretch of country road, 1 stile

LANDSCAPE: dramatic downland on east side of Cuckmere Valley

PUBLIC TOILETS: at car park

TOURIST INFORMATION: Eastbourne, tel: 01323 411400

THE PUB: The Giants Rest, Wilmington

🛈 Although quite long, this walk is generally easy and suitable for experienced children of all ages

Getting to the start

Wilmington is signposted south off the A27 between Lewes and Eastbourne, 2 miles (3.2km) west of Polegate. Drive through the village to locate the car park on the right at the top of the hill.

Researched and written by:
Nick Channer, David Halford

Wilmington EAST SUSSEX

on the track as it climbs quite steeply. Pass a second **sign and map** for the nature reserve and make for a junction with the **South Downs Way**.

5 Turn left and follow the enclosed path to a gate. Go straight ahead alongside **woodland** and pass through a second gate. The path begins a gradual curve to the left and eventually passes along the rim of a spectacular dry valley known as **Tenantry Ground**. Keep the fence on your left and look for a gate ahead. Swing right as you approach it to a stile and then follow the path beside the fence, crossing the top of the **Long Man**.

6 Glance to your right and you can just make out the head and body of the

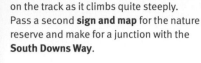

what to look for

Wilmington Priory, by the car park, was founded for the Benedictine abbey of Grestain in Normandy, and much of the present building dates from the 14th century. As few as two or three monks resided here and they used the parish church in Wilmington rather than build their own place of worship. The monks were engaged in managing the abbey's English estates. The priory is in the care of the Landmark Trust and used as a holiday let. It is not open to the public.

chalk figure down below. It's an intriguing view. Continue, keeping the fence on the right, and descend to a **gate**. Turn right here and retrace your steps to the car park at Wilmington.

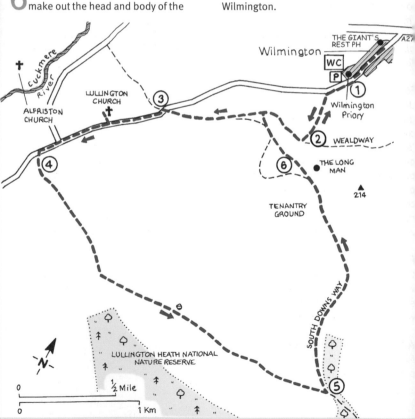

The Giants Rest

The Giants Rest is a tall Victorian building with a comfortably worn interior. It has an informal atmosphere and offers a friendly welcome to walkers. It takes its name from the giant 240ft (73m) Long Man of Wilmington carved into the chalk downland above the village. On cooler days you can relax in the long wood-floored bar on old pews and benches at rustic pine tables. If you're early and lucky, make sure you bag the fireside seats. There are plenty of newspapers to peruse and traditional games to play (there's usually a puzzle or bar game on each table) while you savour an excellent pint – try the award-winning Timothy Taylor Landlord.

Food

Using fresh produce from local suppliers, the menu lists a good selection of home-cooked food. Typically, tuck into warm salads (smoked duck and bacon), whole grilled plaice with herb butter, local sausage ploughman's, home-cooked ham with bubble-and-squeak and home-made chutney, or daily dishes such as wild rabbit and bacon pie or salmon fishcakes with lemon mayonnaise.

Family facilities

Children of all ages are welcome indoors if well behaved. Good summer alfresco seating on the front lawn and rear terrace with super Downland views.

Alternative refreshment stops

Nearby Alfriston offers a good choice of pubs and tea rooms.

about the pub

The Giants Rest
The Street, Wilmington, Polegate
East Sussex BN26 5SQ
Tel: 01323 870207

DIRECTIONS: at the north end of the village, near the junction with the A27

PARKING: 12

OPEN: daily, all day Saturday and Sunday and summer school holidays

FOOD: daily

BREWERY/COMPANY: free house

REAL ALE: Timothy Taylor Landlord, Harveys Sussex, Hop Back Summer Lightning

DOGS: welcome on leads

☛ Where to go from here

Just west of here, visit Drusillas Park, one of the very best small zoos in England (www.drusillas.co.uk). Admire the meerkats, bats, penguins, monkeys and reptiles in naturalistic environments, and take part in activities from gold panning to a train ride through the llama paddock.

A loop from Pevensey to Herstmonceux

A journey between two castles, through the lonely expanse of the Pevensey Levels in '1066 Country'.

At tale of two castles
Pevensey Castle (www.english-heritage.org.uk) has the distinction of being in use for over 1,600 years. In the 4th century the Romans built the large outer

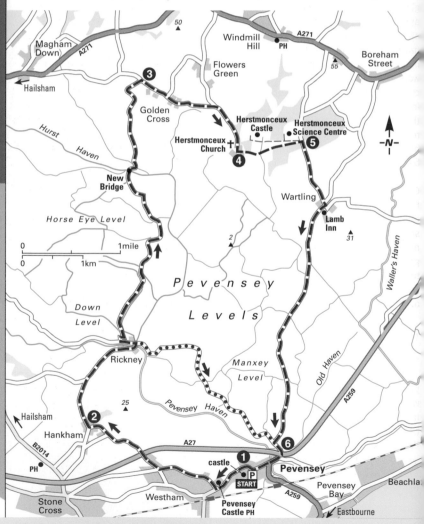

wall you can see from the road. A public footpath leads through the arch from the corner of the road, allowing a view of the Norman castle erected by William the Conqueror, which has an impressively gloomy dungeon, and remains of the keep and chapel. It was attacked many times after the Norman Conquest, and the walls have collapsed at all sorts of odd angles. In the 1940s, during World War Two, it was used as a defence again, and you can see fortifications on the walls. Back in 1076 coins were minted in Pevensey on the site of the 14th-century Mint House, now an antiques shop. It was used as a hideaway by smugglers and is believed to be haunted.

The domes of the former Royal Greenwich Observatory, house the lively Herstmonceux Science Centre (www.the-observatory.org), where you can experience science 'hands on', peering through a microscope, investigating the forces of gravity or touring the telescopes. You can turn your energy into electricity to make a model train run, try out the Bouncing Balls or feel the vibrating effect of the Magic Bowl.

the ride

1 From the car park, go to the main street in Pevensey and turn left along it, passing the outer wall of the **castle** (you can walk in through the gateway, where there is free access, if you don't intend to visit the castle fully later). Just after the **Pevensey Castle pub** turn right along Peelings Lane, ignoring a minor turn soon on the left. Turn right at a crossroads and follow signs to **Hankham**.

2h30 | 13 MILES | 20.9 KM | LEVEL 2

SHORTER ALTERNATIVE ROUTE

1h00 | 5.5 MILES | 8.8 KM | LEVEL 1

MAP: OS Explorer 124 Hastings and Bexhill
START/FINISH: Pevensey car park (by castle; pay and display); grid ref: TQ 646048
TRAILS/TRACKS: all on minor roads, except for an earthy bridleway at Herstmonceux (well-drained but uneven surface, and stepped for a short distance; necessary to push your bike); the short ride is on roads
LANDSCAPE: wetland, waterside, farmland
PUBLIC TOILETS: at the start
TOURIST INFORMATION: Eastbourne, tel: 01323 411400
CYCLE HIRE: MP Cycle Hire, the MasterPiece Studio, the Old Loom Mill, Ersham Road, Hailsham BN27 4RG, tel: 01323 449245
THE PUB: The Lamb Inn, Wartling
🛇 0.75 mile (1.2km) off-road section at Herstmonceux may be muddy and includes steps, where you will have to push. Take care crossing the roundabout outside Pevensey

Getting to the start
Pevensey is just west of the A27 and A259 junction, east of Eastbourne.

Why do this cycle ride?
They may be flat, but the Pevensey Levels are full of colour, character and wildlife, while the South Downs rise dramatically in the background. The ride connects the two contrasting castles at Pevensey and Herstmonceux via a winding, almost traffic-free lane, then a wider road leads down to Wartling and across the Levels to Pevensey.

Researched and written by: Tim Locke

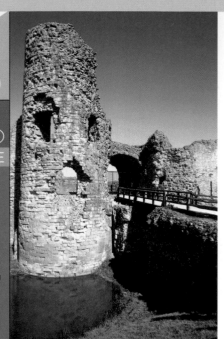

outside. Have a look inside for the tomb of Thomas Lord Dacre (died 1553) and his son Sir Thomas Fiennes. There are also two life-sized marble effigies of knights in armour (not the two Thomases), one with his feet resting on a bright red bulldog, which has a gold crown for a collar.

4 Past the church, where the public road ends, go forward, veering left on the bridleway, and follow blue arrows and waymarkers for the **1066 Country Walk**. This leads over a surfaced area near college outbuildings and a car park, and down through **woodland** (it can be muddy). It then crosses a field, with an excellent view of **Herstmonceux Castle** to the left, a superb brick moated castle begun in 1441 with a gatehouse topped by two towers; it is not always open to the public, so enjoy the view from here. Ahead is one of the **telescope buildings** of the former Royal Greenwich Observatory, from whose atomic clocks the familiar six-pips were originally transmitted to the BBC for broadcast. The observatory, which had to move from Herstmonceux because there was too much light pollution, is now based in the Canary Islands. You need to push your bike up some steps and later you will see the other domes of the **old observatory** (now Herstmonceux Science Centre).

5 Turn right on the road (just to the left is the entrance to the Science Centre and Herstmonceux Castle and grounds) and cycle down to Wartling, keeping right in front of **The Lamb Inn**. Continue for 2.5 miles (4km) back to the edge of Pevensey.

2 Turn right at a T-junction in Hankham, signposted **Rickney**. Keep right at the next junction for Rickney (**National Cycle Route 2**). For a short loop back, at the next junction (in Rickney itself) turn right, then right after 1.5 miles (2.4km). Cross the roundabout and take the road back into **Pevensey**.

For the main ride, turn left at the junction in Rickney (signposted **Hailsham**), then take the first right, signposted **Herstmonceux**. Both the short and full rides have lovely views across the Pevensey Levels, which was once sea. The area eventually filled with shingle, and in medieval times was reclaimed to make farmland. Now it is an important wetland with many bird and flower species.

3 After 3 miles (4.8km) turn right at the next junction and keep right at two more junctions to reach **Herstmonceux Church**; note the mounting block for horse-riders

6 Cross the **roundabout** carefully, using the cycle crossing points, and take the road into Pevensey to return to the start point.

The Lamb Inn

about the pub

The Lamb Inn
Wartling, Herstmonceux
East Sussex BN27 1RY
Tel: 01323 832116
www.lambinnwartling.co.uk

DIRECTIONS: on the road between
Pevensey and the A269 (from the A269, turn
off just east of Windmill Hill, signposted
Pevensey and Wartling)
PARKING: 22
OPEN: daily; all day Saturday and Sunday
FOOD: daily
BREWERY/COMPANY: free house
REAL ALE: Harveys Best, Badger Best,
guest beer

The 17th-century Lamb Inn underwent
extensive refurbishment in 2003 and
now draws discerning pub-goers across
the marshes for imaginative pub food,
good wines and a civilised atmosphere.
Beyond the chatty locals' bar, with its
wood-burning stove, there's a beamed
snug bar, with a brick fireplace and old
wooden tables topped with chunky
church candles. More candles and
flowers decorate the smart lounge,
where you can relax in deep sofas and
armchairs while studying the interesting,
weekly changing blackboard menu,
before dining in the spacious, yet cosy,
warmly decorated restaurant.

Food

Local produce is a feature of the menu,
which often includes rod-and-line caught
halibut with pea pesto, Seaford Bay scallops
and pancetta, and shank of South Downs
lamb stuffed with spinach and Stilton.
Further choices are home-made burgers
and pies, sausage and mash, confit of
duck, tasty soups and puddings such as
lemon bread-and-butter pudding.

Family facilities

Children are allowed in the eating area
of the bar and there's a children's menu
available. The super back terrace has
flower tubs, a pond and fountain.

Alternative refreshment stops

Castle Cottage Restaurant next to the
entrance to Pevensey Castle, and there are
The Smugglers and Pevensey Castle pubs
in Pevensey.

☛ Where to go from here

Eastbourne (www.eastbourne.org/tourism),
is a handsome seaside resort. The Museum
of Shops has a collection of 100,000 shop
items. The Miniature Steam Railway Park
features one-eighth-scale steam and diesel
trains that take you round a lake.

From Winchelsea to Rye and beyond

Two historic gems, and a castle in between, plus the biggest and best sandy beach in the south east.

Winchelsea and Rye

Today Winchelsea seems an idyllic sleepy village, yet in medieval times it was one of the prosperous 'Cinque Ports' – Channel port towns that supplied ships and men to the navy. It was built in the 13th century in a grid plan after the old town at the foot of the hill was washed away in a storm. Black Death and attacks from the French led to lean times over the next two centuries, and much of it was rebuilt later on; many houses still have vaulted cellars (some visible from the street) for storing wine, and there are three town gateways. The church stands partly incomplete, partly ruined, but inside it is grandly proportioned, with fine canopied tombs. Visit the Court Hall Museum for the full story.

Similarly lost in time, Rye was another Cinque Port, stranded inland as the sea has receded. Its knot of hilly streets, including cobbled Mermaid Street with its ancient Mermaid Inn, has a delightful array of tile-hung, timber-framed and brick buildings. The Landgate and Ypres Tower are medieval fortifications, and don't miss the glorious view from the top of the church tower. The Rye Castle Museum looks at the town's past.

*he cobbled road and plant-festooned buildings
) Rye's Mermaid Street*

he ride

1 With the New Inn on your left and the
churchyard behind you, take the road
head to the **A259 sign**, turn right towards
`ye and soon descend steeply. Take the
`rst left, signposted **Winchelsea Station**,
s the road hairpins sharp right. After the
evel crossing (stop and wait if the light is
ed), turn right at the T-junction on **Dumb
Voman's Lane**. As the road starts to bend
eft uphill take the bridleway through the
`ate ahead (signposted **National Cycle
Route 2**). This goes along the foot of what
ised to be sea cliffs in Roman times.

2 Turn right by a **pumping station** (with
green turrets), avoiding the road ahead
near houses, on a permissive cycle path to
each **Gibbet Marsh car park**. Keep right to
kirt the car park (if you are starting from
nere, take the path at the back of the car
ark, near the **picnic benches**, and turn
eft). The path bends right, opposite a
windmill**, and crosses the railway line. You
vill later return to Winchelsea by following
:he road to the right, but first go left and
`ound to the right into **Rye town centre**,
wheeling your bike through town. Visit the
:ourist information centre/Rye Heritage
Centre/Town Model, then turn left and go
up cobbled **Mermaid Street**. Turn right at
:he top along West Street, then right and
eft to skirt the right side of the churchyard.
`n front of Ypres Tower, turn left, then right,
soon passing **Rye Castle Museum**. Turn
right at the next junction, and just before

MAP: OS Explorer 125 Romney Marsh
START/FINISH: New Inn, Winchelsea (free
roadside parking near the pub and church);
grid ref TQ 904174. Alternative start: Gibbet
Marsh car park, Rye; grid ref: TQ 915203
TRAILS/TRACKS: roads, surfaced cycle
paths, stony in places, grass track: mountain
bikes recommended
LANDSCAPE: farmland, coast
PUBLIC TOILETS: Winchelsea, Rye,
Camber Sands
TOURIST INFORMATION: Rye,
tel: 01797 226696
CYCLE HIRE: Rye Hire, Rye, tel: 01797
223033; Sundays and bank holidays
tel: 01797 227826
THE PUB: The New Inn, Winchelsea

🛈 Short sections on main road. Take care
with road crossings in Winchelsea and Rye.
Cross the railway with care at Winchelsea
Station and at Rye. Wheel your bike through
Rye when going in the Camber direction.
One steep hill up into Winchelsea

Getting to the start

Winchelsea is signposted off the A259
between Rye and Hastings. You can also start
at Rye: use Gibbet Marsh car park signposted
from the B2089.

Why do this cycle ride?

Apart from the little hills on which the Rye
and Winchelsea stand, this is a level route
from Winchelsea to Camber Sands, and a
more demanding close to Camber Castle.

Researched and written by: Tim Locke

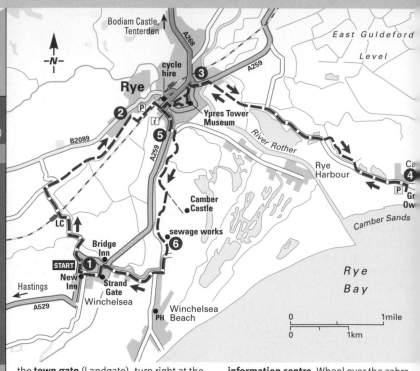

the **town gate** (Landgate), turn right at the end of the railings, go down a path and over a zebra crossing, then left through the car park and right through the park to join the pavement by the **A259**.

3 At a **bike symbol** you can now ride your bike again, along the pavement and over the A259 river bridge. Turn right on the other side on the **bike path**, signposted to Camber. This later crosses the road by a traffic island. After 2 miles (3.2km) the bike path ends by **houses**.

4 Cross the road, enter the car park and take the path over the dunes and on to **Camber Sands**. Return the same way to Rye: wheel your bike over the zebra crossing and up the path to the Landgate. Cycle left along Rye's main street, ignoring side turns, and drop downhill to reach a junction of roads. Take the road ahead (the continuation of Mermaid Street) to reach the **tourist**

information centre. Wheel over the zebra crossing away to your right and follow the A259 towards **Hastings** (cycling along the road or wheeling along the pavement).

5 Turn left, signposted **Rye Harbour**, over the canal, then turn right on a bridleway. At the next house, fork left through a gate. The route follows a raised **grassy dyke**. At a junction near **concrete sheds**, with Camber Castle ahead, keep right in the direction of the blue arrow (or leave your bike here and walk along the path to see the castle). The track is fainter and bumpier, following a slight ridge.

6 By a **sewage works** join a concrete road, then keep forward along a tarmacked road. Turn right on a larger road, left on the A259, and left up a steep road into **Winchelsea**. Go under Strand Gate and keep forward to reach **The New Inn**.

The New Inn

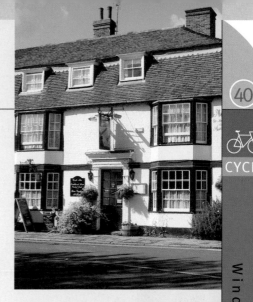

The comfortably old-fashioned, 18th-century New Inn is opposite the church in the centre of this ancient town. The cosy, rambling interior has three bustling beamed rooms, all sporting nice old furnishings and good warming winter log fires. There's a separate locals' bar, well-kept Greene King ales and simply furnished bedrooms with delightful views. An inviting walled garden to the rear of the pub is perfect for alfresco meals or simply to relax in following an energetic walk or cycle ride.

about the pub

The New Inn
German Street, Winchelsea
East Sussex TN36 4EN
Tel: 01335 370396

DIRECTIONS: The New Inn is opposite the church in the middle of Winchelsea

PARKING: 20

OPEN: daily; all day

FOOD: daily; all day Sunday

BREWERY/COMPANY: Greene King

REAL ALE: Greene King IPA and Old Speckled Hen, Morland Original

ROOMS: 6 en suite

Food

You can order home-made pies, roast chicken, a range of steaks with sauces, and hearty snacks such as sandwiches and ploughman's lunches from the printed menu. The special board includes local fish such as whole Dover sole and red mullet alongside lamb shank in red wine, and minced beef and onion pie.

Family facilities

Well-behaved children are allowed in the bar area and restaurant, where young children can choose from a standard kid's menu.

Alternative refreshment stops

There's the Tea Tree (tea room) and the Bridge Inn at Winchelsea, plus a full range of cafés, restaurants, pubs and shops in Rye, and cafés and the Green Owl pub in Camber.

☛ Where to go from here

Fifteen miles (24.1km) north west of Rye is Bodiam Castle (www.nationaltrust.org.uk), a fairytale, 14th-century ruin surrounded by a moat. The walls stand to their original height, and there are staircases and turrets to climb. You can reach it by riding a steam or diesel train on the Kent and East Sussex Railway (www.kesr.org.uk) from just outside Tenterden, a rewarding little Wealden town with many weatherboarded houses.

Acknowledgements

The Automobile Association would like to thank the following photographers, establishments and photo library for their assistance in the preparation of this book.

Photolibrary.com front cover b.
David Foster 47, 63, 71, 103; David Hancock 22, 23, 27, 31, 33, 34, 35, 78, 79, 99, 119, 129b, 131; David Halford 90, 91t, 91b, 115, 125, 127, 129b, 131, 139, 151, 167; Tim Locke 108, 109, 111, 135, 141, 143, 144/5, 147, 156, 159, 161, 163, 171, 175; Peter Toms front cover cr, 39, 43, 59, 67, 93, 95, 107, 118, 123t, 123b.
Anchor Inn, Chideock 19.

The remaining photographs are held in the Automobile Association's own Photo Library (AA World Travel Library) and were taken by the following photographers:

Peter Baker 21, 25, 28/9, 37, 105, 112, 129t, 148, 164/5; E A Bowness 12; Derek Croucher 84/5, 89, 96, 97; Rick Czaja 16; Derek Forss front cover ccr, 24, 52, 53, 55, 61, 92, 104; Max Jourdan front cover cl, 8/9, 36, 41; Tom Mackie 15; S & O Mathews 64/5, 113, 117; Simon McBride 68; John Miller 126, 134, 136/7; David Noble 172; John O'Carroll 50; Tony Souter 14b, 72, 77, 80/1, 121, 133; Martin Trelawny 157; Wyn Voysey front cover ccl, 4, 13, 14t, 44, 45, 51, 56, 73, 75, 83, 85b, 87, 101, 102, 120, 152, 155.